CIARA WOODS

Everything you need to know at work

A complete manual of workplace skills

Prentice
Hall

BUSINESS

an imprint of **Pearson Education**

London • New York • Toronto • Sydney • Tokyo • Singapore • Hong Kong • Cape Town

New Delhi • Madrid • Paris • Amsterdam • Munich • Milan • Stockholm

PEARSON EDUCATION LIMITED

Head Office:
Edinburgh Gate
Harlow CM20 2JE
Tel: +44 (0)1279 623623
Fax: +44 (0)1279 431059

London Office:
128 Long Acre
London WC2E 9AN
Tel: +44 (0)20 7447 2000
Fax: +44 (0)20 7447 2170
Website: www.business-minds.com
          www.yourmomentum.com

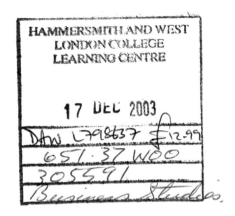

First published in Great Britain in 2003

© Pearson Education Limited 2003

The right of Ciara Woods to be identified as Author of this Work has been asserted
by her in accordance with the Copyright, Designs and Patents Act 1988.

ISBN 0 273 66163 9

British Library Cataloguing in Publication Data
A CIP catalogue record for this book can be obtained from the British Library

10 9 8 7 6 5 4 3 2 1

Designed by Claire Brodmann Book Designs, Lichfield, Staffs
Typeset by Pantek Arts Ltd, Maidstone, Kent
Printed and bound in Great Britain by Ashford Colour Press, Hants

The Publishers' policy is to use paper manufactured from sustainable forests.

Everything
you need to
know at work

Books that make you better

Books that make you better. That make you *be* better, *do* better, *feel* better. Whether you want to upgrade your personal skills or change your job, whether you want to improve your managerial style, become a more powerful communicator, or be stimulated and inspired as you work.

Prentice Hall Business is leading the field with a new breed of skills, careers and development books. Books that are a cut above the mainstream – in topic, content and delivery – with an edge and verve that will make you better, with less effort.

Books that are as sharp and smart as you are.

Prentice Hall Business.
We work harder – so you don't have to.

For more details on products, and to contact us, visit
www.business-minds.com
www.yourmomentum.com

Thank you...

for buying this book.

I'd also like to thank Alessandra Cadorna, Claire O'Donovan, Edward Cahill, Joan Casey, Lesley Felce, Lorna Lynch, Patrick Woods, Rachael Stock, Rachel Russell, Rosita Agnew, Tara Cox, Thomas Woods and Will Eliot for their advice and encouragement.

And finally, a special thank you to my mother for her inspiration and my father, without whom I might never have completed this.

Contents

Introduction

I did not have much experience of working in an office environment before my first job. Despite having studied at a top business school I found myself largely unprepared for the practicalities of working life. I seemed to learn a lot of very important things *accidentally* because I *happened* to see someone doing something or because someone *happened* to tell me something. It made me begin to wonder why a lot of the unwritten rules of working in an office environment were not written down. This would surely save a lot of wasted time, energy and embarrassment!

In addition to this knowledge gained from first hand experience and interviews with friends and colleagues I have tried to distil the wealth of information that has been written down in text books. There are a lot of business books out there which cover some of the most theorized and talked about work issues – working in teams, facilitating meetings and preparing presentations – but who has time to read them all?

I have structured the book in a way that each chapter is a stand-alone piece, dealing with a particular topic. Within the chapter the topic is broken down into various sub-topics. In this way, it should be easy for you to quickly identify where there is information on a particular topic of interest and then read only that. Indeed the book is written so people can dip in and out of it, rather than reading it in a sequential manner – although feel free to do this if you so wish.

Finally, I would say that although there are accepted ways to work in an office environment, remember who you are and keep your individuality. This is not a manual to create an army of company robots but is rather a handbook to help you excel in a corporate environment.

PART **I**

THE
BASICS

- ➡ Meeting and greeting
- ➡ Office technology
- ➡ Correspondence
- ➡ Meetings

CHAPTER 1

Meeting and greeting

➡ Networking

➡ Making conversation

➡ Overcoming problems

➡ On the phone

Many of us meet new people virtually every day of our working lives: customers, suppliers, colleagues, potential business partners and others. And it it a well-known fact that people will make snap judgements and form opinions within minutes of meeting. It's crucial to make a positive first impression – professional, confident and likeable. Whatever opinions are formed about you initially will last a very long time so it makes sense to get off on the right foot. This chapter outlines who you need to know and who to avoid. It also gives tips on making small talk, remembering names and being a good listener before giving advice on how to deal with the most common communication-related problems. Finally it has a section that deals with making phone calls, leaving voicemails and answering the phone.

Networking

You are not alone if you see networking (developing contacts and acquaintances throughout organizations and across industries) as something negative. However, you will never succeed in your chosen career if you float around on your own. It is absolutely essential to be tuned into what's happening in your industry and your company, so think of networking as a necessity. Try to seize every opportunity to meet new people – you never know, you may even make some great friends!

1. **Initiate contact.**
   - Find a way of meeting the person. You could send an email, call them up or ask someone to introduce them to you.
   - Try to find common ground and areas of shared interest.
   - Think of what you could do to help them, rather than just focusing on how they may be able to help you.

2. **Maintain your contacts.**
   - Keep a record of the names and addresses of your contacts (as well as other useful information).
   - Keep in contact by inviting them to special events, sending articles that may be of interest or your congratulations if you hear of an engagement, birth of a child or a major promotion.
   - Keep any promises you make. Respond to requests quickly and be reliable in every way. When you do something for someone, do so with no strings attached.

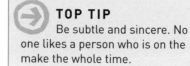

TOP TIP
Be subtle and sincere. No one likes a person who is on the make the whole time.

TOP TIP
In the very early stages of your job, you will get the chance to meet senior people whom you might not normally encounter in the course of your work. Don't waste this opportunity by being afraid to say something. No gushing introduction is necessary; just a simple, confident 'hello' will suffice.

Who you need to know

When starting a new job you should make it your business to meet your peer group, your boss, your boss's boss, people from other depts and human resource reps. As you settle into your role, meeting people will continue to be important and your networking skills will need to be well honed. There is no need to see every person you know in terms of some sort

TOP TIP
Don't underestimate the power of secretaries or Technical Support.

of transaction, but you can make life easier for yourself by ensuring you spend time with certain people and avoid others.

Essential contacts

✓ People in support roles.
✓ People who make things happen.
✓ People who give you advice, support and feedback.
✓ People who provide access to information.
✓ People who provide introductions to others.
✓ People who do or could help your cause.

People to avoid

✗ People who talk too much.
✗ People who are extremely competitive and at your job level.
✗ People who have a negative attitude about the company, job and employees.
✗ People who drag you down.
✗ People you can't trust.
✗ People who stress those around them.

Try to get a mentor at work but don't depend too much on formal mentors who may be assigned to you – they often do not work out. Try to find someone you get on with (who has influence) who will act as an informal mentor to you.

TOP TIP
Don't trust anyone who tells you something 'in confidence', especially something they promised to keep secret.

Making conversation

Introducing yourself

Try to be as open and as friendly as possible to all the people you meet. Don't worry too much about how to introduce yourself, just make sure the introduction is made. Even if you know the person already, you should still shake hands.

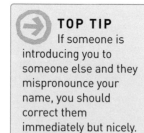

TOP TIP
Limp handshakes are a major turn-off for most people. The trick is to squeeze the other person's hand firmly and shake their hand two or three times from the elbow (not the wrist). The handshake should be calm, not energetic.

The handshake

- Always stand up or move towards the person as they approach (even if they say not to get up).
- Smile and extend your hand to shake theirs.
- Maintain eye contact with the other person throughout.

The introduction

- Introduce yourself in a clear, non-apologetic voice.
- Introduce yourself by your first and last name. You may introduce yourself by your first name only to your peers in informal settings.
- Have a brief résumé about yourself ready (e.g. where you have come from, university/last job, what your role is and who you will be working with) in case people ask.

Group introductions

If you start your job at the same time as a number of others, you will probably have to sit in a big circle and introduce yourself. This can be quite daunting, as there is pressure to be funny but friendly. It is something that you have to get used to as training courses provide more opportunities for group introductions. To make the introductions more interesting, you are often asked to tell something about yourself so be prepared for the following scenarios:

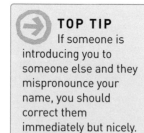

TOP TIP
If someone is introducing you to someone else and they mispronounce your name, you should correct them immediately but nicely.

TOP TIP
The key is to sound confident, make eye contact with everyone and be brief.

- An interesting fact/story about yourself.
- Your most embarrassing incident.
- Five words that describe you.
- What your hobbies are.
- If you weren't doing this job, what you would do.

Tips for remembering names

Make a special effort to remember people's names. People are always impressed when someone remembers their name. It sends out a signal that they are valued and important. It can also prevent embarrassing situations where you need to introduce them to someone and have to let them know you have forgotten their name.

1. **Listen carefully to the name the first time your hear it.**
   - Make a conscious effort to concentrate on the person's name when the person says it for the first time. Do not be distracted by other things; just listen carefully to their name and make a mental note of it.
   - Ask for it to be repeated if you didn't hear the name distinctly (e.g. 'Sorry, I didn't get your name clearly').

2. **Fix it in your mind.**
   - Remark on it, if it is an unusual name (e.g. 'That's a lovely name, how is it spelt?' 'Where is it from?' or 'How should I pronounce it?').
   - Make a visual connection between the person's name and something about them (preferably something that won't change, e.g. not their red jumper).
   - Repeat the name several times at the beginning of the conversation until you have absorbed it. Repeat it again when you say goodbye.
   - Write down the names of the people you have met after every encounter. Seeing a name written down will help you to remember it.

3. **Ask if you can't remember it.**
   - If you genuinely can't remember the name, it is best to ask again as soon as possible.
   - If you are too embarrassed to admit you can't remember, a good trick is to suggest exchanging business cards.

> **TOP TIP**
> Don't accept that you are 'dreadful at remembering people's names'. Work at being good at it. It's an extremely important skill and one at which you can improve.

Small talk

Once you have made your introduction, don't stand there saying nothing; make small talk! It isn't always easy, but here are some fail-safe rules:

Always make the other person feel important

- You may have a burning desire to talk about something but becoming interested in other people is an easier way to build relationships than trying to get other people to be interested in you. Everyone has a subject that they enjoy talking about – you just need to figure out what it is.

Try to find some common ground

- Try to find a shared interest (e.g. a country you have both visited or an exhibition you both saw) and always focus on the similarities between you rather than the differences.

 TOP TIP
People are usually far more interested in their own lives than they ever will be in yours.

Keep it appropriate

- There are certain topics that are regarded as taboo when meeting someone in a business context.

 CHECK LIST Appropriate and Inappropriate Topics

✓ Your journey there	✗ Marital status (including divorce)
✓ Cultural or sporting events	✗ Health
✓ Books, films, magazine or newspaper articles	✗ Personal finance (including salary)
	✗ Rude or racist remarks
✓ Happy occasions (e.g. weddings or births)	✗ Most jokes
✓ General business events or news	

Keep it sincere

- It may sound paradoxical, but the key to good small talk is sincerity. Most people recognize insincerity, so be sincere when speaking with everyone. Keep the conversation light and pleasant, always look interested and avoid too much flattery.

TOP TIP
If you want people to enjoy meeting you, you need to have a good time meeting them. Don't worry, though, the more you do it, the easier it gets.

How to be a good listener

Being a good listener is extremely underrated as people view it as submissive. Most people believe that talking is a better way to establish their worth. However, the best conversationalist is usually a good listener and having strong listening skills can prove very powerful. In order to improve your listening skills, try to:

Give the other person a chance to speak

- Give at least half of the conversation time to the other person.
- Ask their opinion with open-ended questions if they need encouragement.

Give your undivided attention

- Stay focused on what is being said. Don't get distracted by the person's appearance, accent, a fly buzzing or a nearby conversation.
- Don't use your listening time to prepare your response.
- Don't interrupt other than to ask a question or to make sure you understand what they are saying by paraphrasing what you heard.
- Schedule a time with them if you don't have time to listen.

MIND YOUR MANNERS!

It is extremely rude to look over someone's shoulder as they speak to you.

Listen actively

- Listen with your mind and your eyes. Listen 'between the lines' for what is really being said. Watch the speaker's body language.
- Be able to name all the key points the person made, after the conversation.
- Make a conscious effort to listen for the emotional content of what is 'unspoken'.

Listen with an open mind

- Avoid preconceptions about the person who is speaking and avoid premature evaluation. Never assume you know what is going to be said.
- Look for areas of agreement rather than differences.
- Don't argue in your head and don't get emotive or defensive.
- Try to avoid selective hearing.

Show that you are listening

- Make eye contact with the speaker. Don't just pretend to listen.
- Be supportive and encouraging about what they are saying.

TOP TIP

Empathy is the key to being a good listener. Always try to see things from the speaker's point of view.

Overcoming problems

Getting people to listen

- Be confident.
- Keep what you have to say brief and to the point.
- Believe in what you are saying.
- Make eye contact but don't stare.
- Vary your voice to keep people interested.
- Get people involved by asking them questions.
- Bring your conversation alive with examples, quotes, humour and stories.

 CHECK LIST Positive and Negative Speaking Manner

✓ Be assertive when expressing ideas and opinions.
✓ Speak in a controlled and measured way.
✓ Project your voice when in a group.
✓ Pay attention to your ennunciation, diction and grammar.

✗ Don't express self-doubt in a public forum.
✗ Don't mumble.
✗ Don't laugh nervously and uncontrollably.
✗ Don't use slang, nicknames or swear words.

Managing whom you speak to

There will always be people you are dying to speak to and those you are dying to avoid. The key is not to make either desire too obvious.

Getting to speak to someone you want to:

- Watch for an opportunity when the person you want to meet is alone or approachable. Don't make a beeline and don't look over-eager. Be polite to those you pass on the way but don't get caught up in conversations.

Avoiding speaking to someone you don't want to:

- Go through the standard introductory formalities, if someone you are not interested in approaches you, say hello, but cut off small talk by politely saying, 'If you'll excuse me, there's something I have to attend to, perhaps we could speak again later', smile and make your exit.

> **TOP TIP**
> Making a few meaningful and memorable contacts is usually much more productive than being a social butterfly.

Dealing with snubs

Snubs (when someone is rude to you when you try to make conversation) are an inevitable part of life and should be seen as something that everyone experiences from time to time. If you are snubbed:

Remain calm

- Try to turn the negative remark back on the person who made it, by letting them know how rude their comment was. This can be done by calmly saying 'Really, I'm sorry you think that, could you explain more?'

Forget about it and move on

- The problem with snubs is that by the time you have realized that you were snubbed, the moment to make a good reply has often passed.

Remain above snubbing

- Never intentionally snub someone. Trying to return the snub is lowering your standards.

> **TOP TIP**
> Be yourself. If you act true to yourself, you are in control. If you conform to other people's views, it is they who are in control. Remember, no one can make you feel inferior unless you let them.

> **TOP TIP**
> Never forget that you are not obliged to tell anybody anything. You can even be explicit about it by saying something like 'I'd prefer if we didn't talk about that.' An unanswered question is usually more uncomfortable for the asker than the person asked.

Getting people to open up

At the beginning of a conversation people are usually wary about letting their guard down. You need to find common ground so that you can enter the other person's world, but this is a delicate matter. If you try to barge into their private territory, they will respond by closing up. Instead:

Cultivate ease

- Adopt a relaxed stance, speak respectfully, give the person your exclusive attention and show that you are not trying to compete with them (e.g. don't give information to show off).

Ask for permission to enter their personal territory

- Ask either directly by saying 'Do you mind if I ask you...?' or indirectly, by hesitantly suggesting a topic of conversation by looking away and pausing a lot.

Wait for permission to be granted before forging ahead

- Permission may be granted or refused either explicitly ('I'd rather we didn't talk about this' or by evading the question) or through body language (e.g. nodding and leaning forward or folding arms and avoiding eye contact).

Understanding body language

We are always communicating, even when we stop speaking, as our bodies leak out information about how we are feeling. Often we let people know things we would rather not, through these nonverbal messages. Body language is harder to control than speech so it is worthwhile becoming more aware of it. Take the time to understand your personal habits and idiosyncratic gestures. This will enable you to practise controlling them and ensure you are always sending out the right signals.

TOP TIP
If you try to read someone's body language, don't interpret messages in isolation from others. Everything is happening at once (eyes, body position) so remember to look at it holistically.

The problem with body language is that it is very ambiguous and can be difficult to read. Meaning can vary according to context, cultural norms and the individual in question (e.g. people who fold their arms are often considered defensive, when they might just be cold). As body language is open to misinterpretation it is worthwhile having a broad understanding of what is considered positive and negative body language.

CHECK LIST Positive and Negative Body Language

✔ Sit or stand up straight.
✔ Keep your body open and facing towards the person you are speaking to.
✔ Hold your head high.
✔ Relax your arms and legs.
✔ Smile.
✔ Make eye contact (unless it is not culturally appropriate).
✔ Respect people's personal space.

✗ Don't tower over someone. Try to get at their level.
✗ Don't hunch when you stand.
✗ Don't slouch when you sit.
✗ Don't stare at the floor.
✗ Don't fold your arms or cross your legs.
✗ Don't scratch your head.
✗ Don't fidget (with your hair, pen or notes).

TOP TIP
Don't underestimate the power of a smile. It makes you appear confident and friendly and people will warm to you.

On the phone

It is incredible how difficult making a call can seem, especially when it is an important call, if we don't know the person we are calling, or if the call is being made in an open plan office.

TOP TIP
Don't put it off, just make the call.

Making calls

Plan before calling

- Think through why you are calling, who the best person to speak to is, and whether you are calling at an appropriate time (especially if it's an international call).
- Make sure you have all the information you need to hand.
- Plan exactly what you are going to say. Keep it brief and to the point ('I am calling to discuss x, y and z'). Don't waffle.

Sound friendly

- Be friendly and courteous to switchboard operators and secretaries (especially to assistants you contact on a regular basis).
- Try to establish a rapport with the person you are calling.

Speak clearly

- State your name and company or department as necessary. You may need to briefly say why you are calling.

MIND YOUR MANNERS!

Personal calls are best avoided in an office environment. If you must make a call, be discreet and brief and make sure you are not disturbing anyone from his or her work.

- Speak slowly and distinctly, ask clear questions and give the other person time to respond. Don't babble.
- Always spell out difficult names clearly and repeat contact numbers.

Control the volume of your voice

- Speak at a level that is loud enough for the person you are calling to hear you, but quiet enough not to disturb others from their work (especially if you are calling from an open plan office).
- Find an empty office where you can make your calls if you have a booming voice and have difficulty controlling the volume.

Be polite

- Always ask if it suits the person to talk to you. If they say they can talk if it is quick, be honest about how quick the call will be.
- Never end a call abruptly. If you are having difficulty ending a call, simply say you have to dash to a meeting and thank the person for their time.
- Always return calls promptly.

Do not underestimate the importance of answering calls properly and leaving messages in a professional manner. Nothing can make a bad impression like a badly answered call or a rambling voice message. There are different things you should have in mind, depending on whose phone you are answering (yours or someone else's). It's not rocket science but it makes all the difference.

Answering the phone yourself

> **TOP TIP**
> If you are not ready to take the call or do not have the information you need at hand, don't waste the person's time. Ask if you could call back in 20 minutes (or later that day).

1. **Don't let a telephone ring more than three times before answering.**

2. **Have a professional greeting.**
   - Don't just say 'hello'. Say something like 'Good morning/afternoon, John Peters speaking'. If you wish, you can also state your company or department name but don't go over the top. Say 'This is Mary Jones', never 'My name is Mary Jones'.
   - Watch your tone of voice. People can pick up on a person's attitude in seconds.

3. **Be helpful.**
   - Deal with the call, if you can deal with it; don't pass it on to someone else.
   - Never get aggressive, even if the other person does.

4. **Make sure you both have a common understanding of any decisions made.**
   - Finish off the call with a quick synopsis of what has been decided and what each one of you must do by when.

> **TOP TIP**
> Email can be an effective way of helping understanding, especially when you are planning to discuss something over the phone.
> - Send an email before a call to give the recipient time to digest the information.
> - Send an email after a call to ensure you both had a common understanding of what is to be done, by whom and by when.

5. **Don't end a call without knowing the caller's name and contact details.**

6. **Let the caller hang up first.**
   - Make sure you don't cut them off in mid-sentence.

Answering the phone for someone else

Answering calls

- Refer to the person by saying 'Hello, John White's line, Sharmi Jones speaking.'

Transferring calls

- Let the caller know you have to transfer them to someone else. Explain why and to whom they are being transferred.
- Always stay with the call until you have connected the caller to someone who can help.
- Explain what the caller has explained to you before putting the call through to someone else. This avoids the caller having to repeat everything again.

Explaining unavailability

- Let the caller know the availability of the person they wish to speak to before asking their name so they do not feel as if they are being screened.

TOP TIP
Learn how to transfer calls before you need to.

- Explain your colleague's absence in a positive and professional light. Under no circumstances should you divulge personal information (e.g. 'They have gone to the doctor', or 'They are not in yet').
- Avoid being vague (don't say they are 'busy' or 'unavailable') or overusing the same excuses ('They are in a meeting'). If you have to say that they are not at their desk, or are with someone, try to give an idea of when they should be available.

Offering help

- Offer to help the person yourself or to transfer them to someone who can help.
- Offer to get your colleague to call them back later.
- Offer to let them stay on line but be realistic about how long they may have to hold and never leave a caller holding for more than 3 minutes. Let them know what is happening and ask them if they wish to continue holding. Always thank callers for holding after returning to the line.

Taking messages

- Note the date and time of the call, the caller's name (make sure it is spelt correctly) and contact details (phone number including area code) and the reason for the call. Try to be as accurate as possible. Read the points back to the caller to make sure they are correct.
- Place the message where your colleague will see it. Always check to see that your colleague did get the message.

MIND YOUR MANNERS!
Never ask the caller to call back.

Leaving voice messages

Planning your message

- Think through what you are going to say before you make the call (writing it down will help).
- Hang up if you are caught by surprise by voicemail. Think through your message and ring again. Don't just leave a rambling message.

Structuring your message

1. **Introduction.** *State:*
   - Your name (and company, if making an external call).
   - Who you are calling (if there was no personal greeting).
   - Where you got their name and number (if this is your first call).
   - The time of the call (e.g. 2 o'clock, Thursday afternoon) and the date if you think that the person does not listen to their voicemail everyday.

2. **Purpose of call.**
   - Give a brief description of why you are calling, before mentioning any details (e.g. 'I have called to discuss X, Y and Z').
   - Say you will send an email with the details if it is a complicated message.

3. **Follow-up.** *State:*
   - What the next steps are (e.g. will you call them, or do you want them to call you back?) at the end of the message.
   - How urgent it is.
   - Your telephone number. This should be repeated.

Brevity and tone

Keep it brief and as natural sounding as possible.

- If you know the voicemail will require more than one message, say so upfront ('This is the first of two voice messages I am leaving you'). If you find you need to continue your voicemail, say so at the end of the first and at the beginning of the second ('This is a continuation voicemail, from Patrick O'Donovan regarding the next team meeting').
- Listen to the message and ensure it is easy to follow. If not, re-record it.

TOP TIP

If you end up playing phone tag, give the person you are trying to contact a time when you plan to call back. If you do this, make sure that you follow through with the call as people get very irritated if they keep their phone-line free for someone who has promised to call but doesn't.

Recording voicemail greetings

Keep it brief

- Give a complete but succinct introduction (e.g. 'You have reached the voicemail of Yasmin Manzoor. I'm sorry I can't take your call now, but please leave your name, number and a brief message after the beep and I will get back to you').
- Make it clear what you want the caller to do.

Keep it up to date

- Let it be known when you will be receiving your messages if you will not be accessing your voicemail for an extended time (e.g. owing to holidays or training). Say how you can be contacted if the message is urgent, or give an alternative contact that could help them in your absence. This will prevent repeat calls and duplicate messages for you and frustration for the caller.
- Remember to revert to the original message when you return.

Keep it cheerful and business-like

- Try to keep it sounding professional but not mechanical. Avoid putting on an unnatural 'telephone voice'; just be yourself.

CHAPTER 2

Office technology

➡ Workstation safety

➡ Tips for basic technology

➡ Introduction to software

➡ Internet and Intranet

Technology has increased our efficiency, enhanced communication, and multiplied exponentially the amount of information to which we have access. It has also increased reliance on support services and ultimately added to the frustration of working in an office. Understanding how all the technology works will make your job easier and help you to work more efficiently. So this chapter will help you to use everyday technology more effectively, cope with software issues, as well as outlining ways to avoid physical problems caused by the use of office technology.

Workstation safety

Sitting at a desk, working on a computer for extended periods of time, can cause great damage to your body unless you take certain precautions.

 CHECKLIST

Make sure that you:

✓ **Sit at your desk properly.**
- Adjust your chair to suit your height and your desk level.
- Sit with your legs perpendicular to the floor.
- Put both feet flat on the ground with your weight spread evenly.
- Keep your knees lower than your hips and do not cross your legs.
- Ensure the small of your back is well supported.

✓ **Watch your posture.**
- Keep your elbows at keyboard level and your wrists relaxed.
- Hold the telephone receiver in your hand. Never hold it in to your ear with your chin and shoulder. This is bad for your neck.

✓ **Take care of your computer screen.**
- Put your computer screen at a comfortable reading distance directly in front of you. Make sure it is at eye level so that you can look straight across to the top of the screen without craning your neck.
- Get an anti-glare cover if there is a glare on the screen.
- Clean the screen regularly.
- Avoid prolonged periods staring at the screen. As a general guideline, look away from the screen for 5 minutes each hour. Use this time to make a call or get a drink.

✓ **Check out any pain immediately.**
- Make an appointment to see a physiotherapist if you encounter severe pains after prolonged use of a computer.
- Have your eyes tested once a year.

Tips for basic technology

The telephone is the most basic and most familiar piece of office technology but phones work in different ways. If you don't know how to use yours, get a guidebook (if there is one) from Human Resources or ask a friendly colleague for a demonstration.

CHECK LIST

Make sure you know how to:

✓ Get an outside line. (Do you need to dial 9 or 0 for an outside line?)

✓ Call the switchboard.

✓ Make an internal call. (Is there a short dial system?)

✓ Forward a call.

✓ Set up and access your voicemail.

✓ Direct all calls to voicemail.

✓ Direct your office phone calls to your mobile.

Mobile phones

Mobile phones have become something of a necessity in the workplace, as people tend to have more flexible working conditions. If you do not have a mobile you may be supplied with one, or encouraged to get one. If you do have one, you need to be very careful how you use it:

Choose a civilized ring

- Although amusing, it is unprofessional to have a novelty ring tone.

Never forget where you are

- Do not treat a friend calling you on a mobile phone any differently to them calling you on a landline. Sometimes people are more relaxed and informal on mobile calls and often forget where they are.

- Never make work-related calls or discuss sensitive work-related issues in public places. It may seem like you're using your time well by making calls while waiting at a bus stop or sitting in a café, but you never know who is listening to your conversation.

Manage interruptions while on another call

- Switch your mobile off (after you have seen who the caller is).

- Alternatively, ask the person on the landline if you can be excused for a brief moment. Answer the mobile, tell the caller that you are on another line and you will call them back. Then go back to your original caller.

MIND YOUR MANNERS!

Always switch your mobile off during meetings, business lunches and when you are away from your desk (if you leave it on your desk).

Conference calls

Conference calls are a great way of conducting meetings when people are at different locations and it is not convenient for them to meet in one place.

Setting up a conference call

1. **Choose a conference call company.**
   - Find out if your company uses a particular conference call company by asking a helpful secretary. If not, look for one in the Yellow Pages.

2. **Book the conference call.**
   - State if you want a typed/tape recording of the meeting (this is not always possible).

3. **Note down the dial-in number and booking reference you are given.**
   - Keep these numbers safely in case you need to make any changes.

4. **Send out the details to the call participants (and their secretaries).**
   - Send out an email with the details of the call (time, name of the chairperson and dial-in-number).
   - Be sensitive to people who have to dial-in from abroad and make sure they are given all the necessary codes.

 CHECKLIST

Tell them:
- ✓ Your name and your company's name.
- ✓ Your account number (if you have one).
- ✓ When you would like to book your call (date and time).
- ✓ How long the call will last.
- ✓ The number of people who will be on the call.
- ✓ The name of the chairperson.

5. **Always cancel your conference call prior to the designated time, if you decide not to use it, otherwise you will still be charged for it.**

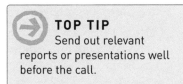 **TOP TIP**
Send out relevant reports or presentations well before the call.

Participating in a conference call

Keep the dial-in details safe

- Make sure you can access the dial-in details when needed.

Book a phone

- Consider booking a conference telephone and an office if you are in the same place as another participant and wish to attend the call together.

Switch off your mobile phone

- Mobile phones create distortion when they ring.

Give your details when you dial in

- Announce your name and those of the other participants who are present with you, if relevant.
- State who the conference chairperson is.

FIX IT!

If you get a bad line:
- Note the number to call or telephone button to press if you encounter problems.
- Re-dial if the problems persist.

Videoconferences

Videoconferences are a great way of conducting meetings when people are at different locations and there is a need to establish rapport that cannot be done over the phone.

Setting up a videoconference

See 'Setting up a Conference Call'

- The procedure is much the same, although videoconferences are usually arranged in-house through the Technology Services department.

Book a videoconference at least a week in advance so that rooms can be reserved

- They tend to take place in specific rooms in most offices so you'll need to reserve the room.
- Choose between a one-way video (only one party can see the other) with two-way audio (the most common) and two-way video with two-way audio.

Participating in a videoconference

Arrive early so that you can familiarize yourself with how it works.

Try to keep your movement to a minimum, as a moving image received on video is often blurred.

Fax

Despite the advent of email, a fax is still a great way to send information. There are a few things you need to bear in mind when using a fax machine:

> **TOP TIP**
> Never assume that the fax has been sent, just because the pages have gone through. Always check the transmission page for confirmation.

- Always write faxes in bold capitals with a pen (pencil will not print clearly).
- Remember that you need to put the paper in face down on most fax machines.
- Check if you need to dial a number (e.g. 9) to get an external line.
- Pay extra attention to the number you dial. Recheck it before pressing 'Send' to avoid sending the fax to the wrong place.
- Avoid faxing on dark coloured paper as it takes a long time to send.

> **MORE INFO?**
> See p.37 for information on writing a fax cover.

- Avoid using faxes for invitations or thank-you letters or when sending highly confidential or contentious information.

Photocopier

In theory, photocopiers are fairly simple tools, however, they can cause great stress. They are becoming increasingly complex machines, offering many different options. It is important to familiarize yourself with the various options and how they work, so that when the time comes, you know how to get the best result. Some photocopiers have a security feature so be aware that you might need a card or code to use the machine.

Some of the most common options are:

- Inserting paper (place pages one at a time on the glass, or multiple pages in the feeder on top)

> **MIND YOUR MANNERS!**
> Never jam a copier and walk away from it for someone else to sort out.

- Paper layout (landscape or portrait)
- Paper type (white, coloured or acetate)
- Making recto verso copies (i.e. copy both sides of the page)
- Document sorting and stapling
- Changing the size (enlarging or minimizing).

> **TOP TIP**
> The photocopier invariably jams when you need to copy something in a hurry for an important meeting, so always give yourself plenty of time.

Printers

The two most frequently used printers are laser and inkjet. While laser printers are much more expensive, they produce higher quality print-outs and tend to be quicker. Most organizations network their printing, so that rather than having your own printer, your computer is attached to a printer on the network that other people will also be accessing.

 FIX IT !

If the printer won't print your page, check if:

- Your computer is correctly connected to the network
- Your page is in a long printing queue (click on the printer icon)
- The printer is plugged in
- The printer has run out of paper
- The printer has run out of toner.

 MIND YOUR MANNERS!

When printing from a networked printer, remember that the printer is not for your sole use. Print large documents in batches of 10–15 pages to allow other people access to the printer.

Scanners

Scanners work like photocopiers. They copy images or text to the computer rather than on a page. The computer needs special software before it can be used with a scanner. Copied items can be manipulated and printed. Scanners are useful for incorporating pictures into presentations or sending articles to a colleague through the Internet.

Overhead projectors

The overhead projector is often used in meetings. You simply place prepared acetates on the overhead and the image is projected on to a screen. Always check that the lens is in focus and that the acetate is the right way up.

Projectors used to project computer images onto a screen can be extremely useful for presentations.

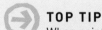 **TOP TIP**
When pointing out something on the slide, use a pen on the actual slide rather than on the screen.

It is not possible to explain how to use the proliferation of devices that exist, but you should always familiarize yourself with the equipment and leave plenty of time before the presentation to make sure it works.

Introduction to software

Most software you encounter in the workplace is based on Microsoft Windows and has very similar screen layout and commands.

The most commonly used Microsoft packages are:

Word

- For word-processing documents.
- The file format for this package is .doc (i.e. so every document you create you will save as a name that ends with .doc).

PowerPoint

- For creating presentations.
- The file format for this package is .ppt

Excel

- For creating spreadsheets.
- The file format for this package is .xls

Access

- For building databases.
- The file format for this is .mdb

TOP TIP

Don't panic! Many 'lost' documents can be found in your temporary files or in the 'bin'.

Problems with software

Writing software is quite complicated and it is extremely hard for the programmer to imagine and cater for every possible user input. It is therefore possible that you can press a combination of keys or a sequence of commands that haven't been catered for by the programmers. If this occurs, the software is said to have a 'bug'. Bugs range from minor annoyances to computer crashes where you lose all of your unsaved data.

FIX IT!

If the computer crashes, try:

- **The CTRL, ALT, DELETE combination**
    - Call up the task list by pressing CTRL, ALT and DEL simultaneously. Click on the problem program and choose End Task. This should allow you to use the rest of the computer.

- **Rebooting**
    - Reboot by pressing CTRL, ALT and DEL twice or by clicking on the start menu and choosing restart.
    - If your computer freezes and you can't reboot, then turn it off by pressing the on/off switch and removing all power supply (including batteries). Leave it off for a minute and then turn it back on.

- **Contacting Technical Support**
    - Rebooting solves most problems, but if it doesn't solve yours, contact your in-house Technical Support. This is a number you should be familiar with and remember to be very nice to the support team!

Viruses

Unlike a bug (which is unintentional), a virus is a hidden set of instructions that are consciously created by hackers to sabotage your system. Viruses are dangerous as they spread silently and often go undetected until they do something bad. The seriousness of the damage ranges from a message appearing on your screen, to infecting a file, to wiping the entire hard disk of information and crippling a network. Viruses usually get into the computer system via disks, Internet downloads and email attachments. Never launch an attachment on an email when you don't recognize the author. Delete the mail immediately.

 FIX IT!

If you have a virus:

- Use a virus-removing program (e.g. Norton Anti-Virus) to clean or delete infected files.
- Copy zipped files in full on your hard drive. Clean the full copy and delete the zipped version as zipped files cannot be cleaned.
- Keep your anti-virus program updated; there are constantly new viruses emerging.
- Empty your trash bin once you have completed the anti-virus check as infected files stored in the trash bin may still cause harm if the files are restored.

Computer security

As laptops can easily be stolen or left in taxis and on trains, it is essential that you use passwords to protect your information. When you are first given your computer, you will probably be given a password but in most cases these can be changed. You will have multiple passwords for different systems and hardware.

 CHECK LIST

You should have a password:

✓ To power on your computer.
✓ On highly confidential documents.
✓ On your screensaver.

When choosing a password, bear the following in mind:

- Choose a password that is easy for you to remember.
- Choose a password that is a combination of alphanumeric and special letters as these are harder to hack into than words or numbers (e.g. instead of using igloo, use 1gl00).
- Update your password by putting a number after the one you already have rather than thinking up and having to remember a new password. Some systems require new passwords every few months.
- Don't write any password down but do record some way of remembering it (e.g. if one is your mother's birthday – write 'mother's birthday' as a reminder, rather than writing the actual date).

Keeping your work safe

Although your computer can be repaired if damaged, or replaced if lost or stolen, your work once lost or corrupt can never be replaced. It is absolutely imperative that you look after your data. If you don't, you may see weeks, even months of work lost in minutes. It is a good idea to:

- Set up Auto Save (from your Control panel).
  - This will automatically save your document every few minutes.
- Save your work after every paragraph and every time you complete an important piece of work.
- Name each document so that you can identify it easily.
- Create folders for each type of work and save relevant documents in each folder.
  - Windows Explorer allows you to sort files by name, size, type and date of last modification. This will put you in control of your work and can help save valuable time.

> **TOP TIP**
> Ensure version control (especially if more than one person is working on the document), by putting a number after the document name (e.g. project(1).doc, then project(2).doc). The highest number should be your most up-to-date version.

> **TOP TIP**
> The storage capacity of a floppy disk can be greatly increased by zipping documents before copying them onto the disk. When you zip documents, you compress them. Zipping packages are standard on most computers.

Storage devices

Information saved on the hard drive can be lost, so it is vital to make back-up copies of the data. If you do this, you will be able to use your information, no matter what happens to your computer. Where you save your data will depend on ease of use and size of storage. The three main storage options are:

- The computer's hard drive (40–900 MBs).
- The network.
  - Set up a personal folder on your office network (if you have one) and save all of your work in it. The server takes a back-up of everything on the network every night, so by saving your work on it, you should always have a recent copy of your work.
- External memory.
  - Diskette   (1.4 MBs)
  - Tape   (4–100 MBs)
  - CD ROM   (650 MBs) Requires a CD writer (or burner).
  - DVD   (5.2 GBs) Requires a CD writer (or burner).
  - Zip Disks   (100MB–2GBs) Requires a zip drive.

Internet and intranet

The Internet is an extremely useful resource, whether used as an information search engine, an email carrier or as a platform for news and chat groups. Check what your company policy on Internet use is and never access inappropriate sites at work.

To access the Internet, you need:

– A modem
– A browser (e.g. Microsoft Internet Explorer or Netscape Communicator)
– An account with a service provider.

 FIX IT!

If your connection is really slow:

- Try dialling up at a time that is less busy (e.g. try not to use local sites first thing in the morning or at lunchtime. Keep in mind the difference in time when accessing foreign sites. If you are accessing US sites from Europe, do so in the morning when America is asleep).
- Consider higher-speed digital services such as an Integrated Services Digital Network (ISDN) line or an Asymmetric Digital Subscriber Line (ADSL). Both these services can be provided by upgrading an existing, conventional telephone line.

The Intranet

An Intranet is similar to the Internet, but has restricted access. Anyone with a computer and a modem can access the Internet but only the employees in a company can access the Intranet as it exists only for company-specific issues and employee-relevant information.

Not all companies have an Intranet, but if your company does, you may need a password to access it. It is worthwhile finding out about as it can be a really useful source of information on the company.

To connect to your work network from home, you need:

– A modem and cable to plug it into the phone socket
– The appropriate office software
– A password to get onto the network.

CHAPTER **3**

Correspondence

➡ Writing well

➡ Tips and templates

While many people are prepared to spend hours working on a report, making sure that it creates the right impression, few give everyday correspondence a second thought. Yet effective correspondence is a key skill in today's work environment and every time you send a letter or an email to someone, your reputation is at stake. Most people have an idea of what sounds right but few are skilled at committing their thoughts to paper. This chapter will give you some advice on how to write well and provides tips and templates for letters, emails, faxes and memos.

Writing well

There is a big difference between literature and business writing; the former is read for pleasure, the latter for information. To write well at work you need to develop your ability to communicate things in a succinct manner. This will save you and your reader time, making life easier for you both.

Spend a few minutes preparing your correspondence

Don't procrastinate, just start somewhere and sort out the logic later

- Don't worry about what to write, just get the words flowing. Write as you speak and wait until you have a first draft (written off the top of your head), before you start editing.

Keep the message brief and to the point

- Structure your ideas so that they flow logically.
- Communicate the most important information first.
- Ensure the message includes everything the person needs to know.
- Make it obvious what the next steps are (e.g. if you will contact them or if they must do something).

 CHECK LIST

Be able to answer the following questions:

✓ **Who is the reader?**
  - How much do they know already?
  - How will they react to the information?

✓ **Why are you contacting them?**
  - Is it to inform, persuade or ask for information?

✓ **What is the one important message that you must get across?**
  - How much do they need to know?

✓ **Where is the information going?**
  - Is this an internal or external communication?
  - Where else could the information end up?

✓ **When do they need this information?**
  - Do they need it by a certain time?
  - Do you need them to respond to you by a certain date?

 TOP TIP

Always keep the layout clean and airy; no one likes to read dense text. If you have a lot to say, summarize the main points on the first page (e.g. a cover letter) and put the detail on a separate page.

Edit with the reader in mind

- Choose the tone and style of the communication so that they appropriately reflect the nature of the subject and your relationship with the reader. For most business correspondence the most effective and appropriate tone is a professional one with a conversational feel.
- Always read through what you have written (from the reader's point of view) when you have finished.

CHECK LIST

To achieve the appropriate tone, keep your writing:

✓ **Warm**
  - Don't depersonalize your writing (e.g. use the pronouns I, we and you).

✓ **Flowing**
  - Create smooth transitions between sentences (e.g. don't be afraid to start sentences with conjunctions such as 'and' or 'but').

✓ **Unpretentious**
  - Use plain, everyday language (e.g. use contractions such as 'I'll' for 'I will') but avoid ending sentences with prepositions (e.g. use 'for whom' rather than 'who ... for').

✓ **Clear**
  - Use short sentences and avoid overusing abbreviations.

✓ **Professional**
  - Be wary of adding humour or resorting to over-used phrases (e.g. 'as a valued customer').

Choose the medium to suit the message

- Use the appropriate technology for the level of formality, confidentiality and speed of response required but don't change your style (you should always aim to say what you have to effectively and efficiently).

CHECK LIST

✓ **If formality is required:**
  - Use: letters, memos
  - Don't use: email, fax

✓ **If a quick response is required:**
  - Use: email, fax
  - Don't use: letters, memos

✓ **If confidentiality is required:**
  - Use: letters, memos
  - Don't use: email, fax

Tips and templates

Tips for letter writing

Format

- Find out what your company's standard format is and use it.
- Use the blocked format (everything is left aligned) if there is no standard.

Opening and closing

- Avoid using 'Dear Sir/Madam'. Try to find out the person's name.
- Use your correspondent's first name only if you know them very well.
- Err on the side of formality if in doubt about the form of salutation.
- Sign off with your full name, even if you open the letter with the person's first name only.
- Handwrite your signature and make it legible.
- Choose an impersonal salutation and complimentary close (e.g. Dear Sir/Yours faithfully) if you use a 'For the attention of' line.

Structure

- *Beginning:* State the purpose of the letter.
- *Middle:* Support this purpose with details and facts.
- *End:* Summarize the situation and outline the next steps.

> **✓ CHECK LIST**
>
> **If you open a letter with:**
> ✓ 'Dear First Name', close with 'Kind regards' or 'Best wishes'.
> ✓ 'Dear Surname', close with 'Yours sincerely'.
> ✓ 'Dear Sir', close with 'Yours faithfully'.

Date

- Write out the date in full (avoid abbreviations, e.g. 'Feb' or '28/2/02').
- Note the date goes before the month in the UK, and after it, in the US.

Tone and humour

- Choose the tone based on the nature of the letter and your relationship with the recipient.
- Never make jokes in a letter, unless you know the recipient well and can guarantee it will be considered funny.
- Never use a postscript (PS) in a business letter.

Address layout for plain paper

Leave two/three lines
Pearson Education Ltd.
128 Long Acre
London WC2E 9AN
+44 (0)20 7447 2000
Leave two/three lines
Your Ref cf/ld
Leave one line
17 June 2002
Leave one line
URGENT
Leave two/three lines
Yellow Company
3 Linchfield Rd
London E1 5SD
Leave two/three lines
Dear Mr Brown,

Paper

- Use company paper only for communicating company business.
- Use a plain second or a continuation sheet rather than a letterhead.
- Make sure you put your (the sender's) address above the recipient's if you use plain notepaper for the full letter.

Final version

- Ensure the letter is easy to read by keeping text neat and paragraphs similar in size. Each paragraph should deal with one point only.
- Take extra care to ensure that the recipient's name, title and address are completely accurate.
- Check your letter for spelling, punctuation and grammatical mistakes. The spell checker on word processors is not always fail safe, so double check.
- Keep a copy of every letter you send.

TOP TIP
Never send anything with errors. If you spot a mistake, start afresh.

Responding to letters

- Reply to a letter within five working days of receiving it, even if it is just to say that you have received the letter and are dealing with it.
- Keep the reference if responding to a letter on the same subject.

Letter template

Pearson Education Ltd.
128 Long Acre, London WC2E 9AN. Tel +44 (0)20 7447 2000

Leave four/five lines
Our Ref fs/tr
Leave one line
Your Ref cf/ld
Leave one line
17 June 2002
Leave one line
FOR THE ATTENTION OF MR L. BROWN
Leave two/three lines
Yellow Company
3 Linchfield Rd
London E1 5SD
Leave two/three lines

Dear Sir
Leave one line

Re SEPTEMBER MARKETING CAMPAIGN
Leave one line
Could you please take a look at the Media Bookings and Ad Schedule that I have enclosed. We need to get them signed off by the end of this week, so if you have any queries please either email me (jeff.goldstein@yellow.com) or give me a call (0207 447 2000). If I have not heard from you by Friday, I will assume that you are satisfied with them.
Leave one line

Yours faithfully,
Leave five/six lines

Jeff Goldstein
Jeff Goldstein
Account Manager

Leave two lines
Encs (1) Media Bookings (2) Ad Schedule

Leave two lines
Copy to John Mansfield, Fiona Bell

Tips for fax cover notes

A fax should always be sent with a one-page cover note. This note ensures that the fax is delivered to the right person and that they know whom to contact and how to contact them if there are any problems (e.g., it is quite common for the recipient to miss a few pages). If you do not have a company fax template, set up your own cover note template using your word processing package. The note should detail:

- The name of the recipient
- Your contact details
- Information about the fax
- A brief note to the recipient.

MORE INFO?
See p.24 for more on sending faxes.

Fax cover note template

Recipient's Details		*Sender's Details*	
To:	**Georgina Holt**	From:	**Anne Woods**
Company:	Yellow Publishers	Tel:	020 7123 4567
Fax:	020 7844 8444	Fax:	020 7234 5678
Date:	1 December 2001		
Subject:	Focus Group Findings		
Status:	Urgent		
Number of Pages:	Cover + 12		

Georgina,

Could you please take a look at the findings from the two Focus Groups and let me know what you think before next Wednesday? I am keen to present the findings to senior management and would appreciate your comments.

If you have any queries regarding them, please don't hesitate to contact me.

Best regards,

Anne

Tips for composing emails

Recipients

- Only send emails to people who need to receive them. Be selective.
- Avoid controversy by listing names alphabetically.
- Think carefully about escalating a problem by cc-ing someone more senior.

Subject line

- Always write a subject line that explains the email (avoid all-purpose headings, e.g. 'Urgent') and that helps the recipient to file it easily.
- The line should encourage the recipient to open the mail.

 CHECK LIST

- ✓ **To:** People to whom the mail is addressed.
- ✓ **cc:** People who need to read the mail, but don't need to act on it.
- ✓ **bcc:** People you would like to see the mail without the original recipient's knowledge. Be careful how you use this.

- Use the same subject message when commenting on the message.

Opening and closing

- As emails are more informal than letters, Mr and Mrs are rarely used.
- Write the recipient's name followed by a comma.
- Sign off with 'Regards', 'Best regards' or 'Many thanks'.
- Set up an automated signature book with all your contact details.

Tone

- Business emails: Friendly but professional.
- Official emails: Require as much thought and gravitas as a letter.
- Social emails: Friendly but never rude or inappropriate.

 MIND YOUR MANNERS!

Avoid:

- SHOUTING (using upper case letters to emphasize a point)
- Spamming (sending out junk or superfluous emails)
- Smileys (use of punctuation marks, e.g. :-), to create a facial expression)
- Flaming (sending a hostile message that is rude or insensitive). If you receive an offensive email, calm yourself down before responding.

Structure

- *Beginning:* Say what you want the person to do and by when (in the first sentence) before going into details. Introduce yourself and say how you got their address, if writing to someone you don't know.
- *Middle:* Support this purpose with details and facts.
- *End:* Summarize the situation and outline the next steps (e.g. they email you back with information or you call them). Make sure it is clear when the action needs to take place.

Content

MIND YOUR MANNERS!

Don't send chain mail or inappropriate attachments to business colleagues. Remember that employers own their email systems and can legally inspect all employees' email.

- Try to include only one message in each email.
- Give reasons for your requests and point out the benefits of doing what you ask.
- Keep the file size down; unnecessary attachments can slow your message.
- Make sure the recipient has the appropriate software and knows how to open the attachments (e.g. right click, launch).
- Never send anything that you would be embarrassed or uncomfortable saying to someone's face. If you are in doubt about the content, don't send it. Once you press the send button, you lose control of the mail and it can be forwarded to anyone, including people you never intended to see it.

Visual effect

- Use both upper- and lower-case letters as it is easier to read than all capital or all lower case letters.
- Keep the message brief. The reader should not have to scroll down to see the whole message.
- Keep paragraphs short. Use headings to separate themes and bullet points to highlight and enumerate key ideas.
- Keep the mail simple. Not all email packages are compatible, so if you try to format your mail (e.g. indents, italics) it may end up distorted.
- Be consistent when using bullet points. Use a dash or numbers.

TOP TIP
Always check your grammar, spelling and punctuation before sending an email.

Email template

Emma Juliet (+44 207 844 8444)
18/04/2000 16:48 GMT

To: jan.adams@pearsoned.com
cc: sharmi.james@pearsoned.com
bcc: david.lee@yellow.com

Subject: New Deadline (17 June)

Jan,

I have just had a look at the project schedule and feel that we will not be able to meet the 31 May deadline. A more realistic target would be 17 June. I understand that this may be a problem for you so please feel free to call me to discuss it.

The reasons for this delay are:
1. The delayed response from our supplier (they took three weeks instead of one).
2. The lack of resource at the beginning of the project (we underestimated the resource required but this has now been rectified).

Let me know what you think.
Best regards,

Emma

Mailbox control

With all the mails you receive daily, your mailbox can easily become disorganized.

CHECK LIST

How to keep control over your inbox:
- ✓ Act on every email immediately (e.g. reply to it, delete it or file it).
- ✓ Don't waste your time opening junk mail; just delete it.
- ✓ Set up folders where you can file emails but be ruthless with what you keep.
- ✓ Make it clear if you don't need an answer to an email.
- ✓ Have specific times when you check your email. Don't let incoming messages be a constant source of interruption.
- ✓ Clear your inbox at the end of every week.

Tips for memos

Memos are often used as a form of internal communication. They can be formal (typed) or informal (handwritten) as the subject matter and audience dictate.

Content

- Give the memo a title and indicate its urgency.
- Start the memo with a short summary of the expected action.
- Use paragraph headings and bullet points where possible.
- Keep it short (preferably not exceeding one A4 page).

Recipients

- Let potential recipients who are on the margin of the circulation list know about the memo and offer them a copy should they want one.

 CHECK LIST

Send a copy to:
- ✓ People who need to take action.
- ✓ People who need to be consulted.
- ✓ People whose seniority makes it courteous or diplomatic to keep them informed.

Top and tailing

- There is no salutation or complimentary closure in a memo.
- There is no need to sign the memo, unless it is very important.

Memo template

Private & Confidential

Meeting

Due to new expense control procedures all taxi bookings must be authorised by Ruth Carroll.

Date: 1 January 2001
Author: Adam Barnes
Contact Details: adam.barnes@handbook.com (020 7123 4567)
Circulation: Marketing Dept.

Sending couriers

Documents often have to be physically sent to different places and if time is of the essence, traditional post might not be quick enough. Couriers bike or fly the papers to their destination in a matter of hours. To send something by a courier:

Find out if your firm uses a particular courier company

- If they do, get their telephone number and your company account number.
- If they don't, look up the Yellow Pages for a nearby courier service.

Stick a courier label on the envelope

- Get a label from a secretary or the stationery cupboard.
- Fill out the name, address and telephone number of the person receiving the parcel.

CHECK LIST

When you call the courier, state:
- ✓ The account number (if you have one).
- ✓ The destination of your parcel (make sure you know the full address, including postcode).
- ✓ The name of the addressee and his/her contact number.
- ✓ When you want it delivered.
- ✓ Where they can pick up the parcel.

TOP TIP
Always address the parcel to a person, rather than a department. If you are not sure to whom you should send the parcel, ring and find out the name of someone who would accept the parcel on behalf of the department.

CHAPTER 4

Meetings

➡ Organizing made easy

➡ Contributing to meetings

➡ Pre-empting and overcoming problems

➡ Surviving business lunches

Meetings, be they formal or informal, prearranged or impromptu, are an essential part of working life. However, far too many meetings are unproductive and a waste of time. Mastering the skills of chairing, recording and attending meetings early on in your career will save you a lot of time and frustration and will also enhance your reputation. This chapter covers everything you need to know about organizing, chairing and attending meetings. It also gives tips on taking minutes and exchanging business cards as well as making suggestions for overcoming some of the most common problems associated with meetings. Finally, there is a section on the etiquette of business lunches.

Organizing made easy

If you have to organize a meeting, work through the following issues:

Objective

- Decide the main purpose of the meeting (e.g. to solve a problem, make a decision or collect information) and communicate it to the attendees.

Attendees

- Invite people who will contribute to the topics under discussion.
- Try to limit the number of attendees to about seven.
- Confirm attendance two days before the meeting.

Agenda

- Outline the specific topics to be discussed and questions to be answered.
- Prioritize each of the issues and allocate a certain amount of time to them. Be realistic about what you can achieve.
- Send out the agenda well before the meeting takes place. People should be given time to collect their thoughts about decisions that need to be made.

Location

- Choose somewhere that is convenient for everyone (not just you).
- Don't have important meetings in your office, as you will be unable to avoid interruptions or get rid of people when it is over.
- Allow time for "over-run" when you book the room.

Requirements

- Organize projectors, flip charts and screens as required.
- Order beverages and biscuits/sandwiches as necessary.
- Provide reception with a list of visitors at least 24 hours before they are expected. Ask reception to prepare nametags if appropriate.

Time

- Hold meetings before lunch if you want them to be brief.
- Do brainstorming sessions early in the morning.

 CHECK LIST

Check the room to ensure that:
- ✓ It is big enough.
- ✓ It is not too hot or too cold (if it is, speak to building services).
- ✓ There are enough chairs.
- ✓ The layout is appropriate (if not, rearrange the room to suit the meeting but when the meeting is over make sure you leave it the way you found it).

Business cards

Always carry business cards with you but be careful where, when, how and to whom you hand them out. Believe it or not, there is etiquette to giving out your business cards.

Remember, business cards reflect on you personally

- Keep your cards clean and flat. Never hand out a grubby or bent card.
- Always 'present' the card with the text facing the receiver so that they can read it.

Don't be too eager to hand your cards out

- Follow the lead of the meeting chairperson. He/she will usually exchange cards either at the beginning of the meeting, when you are being introduced, or at the end, when the next steps are being discussed.

TOP TIP

Always have cards with you in business situations but never give them out indiscriminately. See your business card as an item of value, not a disposable piece of paper.

Assess the appropriateness of the situation before handing out a card

CHECK LIST

Distribution – Dos & Don'ts

✓ Someone asks you what you do.	✗ You are in a social situation (unless someone specifically asks for one).
✓ You are making acquaintance with people for the first time at a formal meeting.	✗ If a personal card would be more appropriate.
✓ Someone asks for your contact details for business purposes.	

Pre-empting and overcoming problems

Lack of structure

- Circulate the agenda well in advance.
- Explain how the meeting will be run and assign roles at the beginning.

TOP TIP
Short, frequent meetings are good, unnecessarily long ones are bad.

Bad use of time

- Start and end meetings on time and don't wait for latecomers.
- Assign a realistic portion of the time to each item and stick to the timing. Get someone to be a timekeeper, if necessary.

People contributing

- Ask people to confirm attendance before the meeting so that you can ensure all the important people will be present. If someone crucial can't make it, try to convince them that it is important or reschedule.
- Try politely to prevent any one person talking too much.
- Direct questions to people who are not getting involved.

All talk, no action

- Make a clear and final decision on everything on the agenda.
- Assign responsibility for completing each task and set a deadline.
- Ensure everyone understands what is expected.
- Review the progress at the next meeting.

CHECK LIST

Common Buzzwords
- ✓ Book time in the diary (schedule an appointment).
- ✓ Bring up to speed (brief someone).
- ✓ Keep in the loop (keep someone informed).
- ✓ Push the envelope (try something new).
- ✓ Singing from the same hymn sheet (everyone understands the same thing).
- ✓ Thinking outside the box (think about things differently).
- ✓ Touch base (speak/get together to discuss the status).

Overuse of buzzwords

- Try to manage your use of buzzwords as speaking only in buzzwords can become quite tedious. However, although they are often overused, they can sometimes be useful.

Nerves

- Take deep breaths and speak slowly. Consciously work at appearing relaxed and confident and try to contribute to the discussion.
- Remember that all the people are human. Imagine them doing something mundane, and then they will not seem so intimidating.

PART

II

THE

SKILLS

➡ Problem solving

➡ Research

➡ Financial awareness

➡ Presentations

5

Problem solving

➡ The process

➡ Lessons learned through experience

➡ Tried and trusted techniques

You might feel that a lack of knowledge and experience is a stumbling block in solving a problem, but it can often be a huge advantage. When solving problems, imagination is just as important as information, so make use of your fresh approach and your lack of assumptions about the way things should be done. Often, challenging an assumption can turn obstacles into opportunities. Seeing things differently is a key skill and this chapter will give you the structure to feel confident enough to unleash your creativity. It will also outline some things you should bear in mind when solving a problem, as well as suggesting some useful problem-solving techniques.

The process

Before you start to solve a 'problem', ask yourself two things: first, is there really a problem? And second, should you be trying to solve it?

- If there is no real problem why waste time trying to solve it? This may sound obvious, but it is amazing how many people do waste time.
- If there is a problem, you may not be expected to solve it or you may not have the time to. Maybe it's not you who should be solving this particular problem.

If you decide you should and can solve the question at hand, the following process should help:

1. **Identify the problem.**
   - Write down a description of the problem, answering all the who, why, what, where, when and how questions. Although this description may evolve over time, if you can state your problem in a clear and concise way, then you are halfway to solving it.
   - Don't get bogged down in understanding the cause of the problem at this early stage, as it is often very hard to discern.
   - Show your description of the problem to someone who is affected by it. Check with them that you have correctly understood it.

2. **Write down all the possible solutions.**
   - Think of as many ways of solving the problem as you can.
   - Ask other people what they think. Brainstorming is a fantastic way to generate lots of ideas in a short space of time. (See Techniques section.)
   - Try to be as specific and realistic as possible about proposed approaches.

3. **Evaluate each of these options.**
   - Look at each option from different perspectives. De Bono's Hats is a great way to do this. (See Techniques section.)
   - List the pros and cons for each option.
   - Eliminate options that don't make the grade or are unrealistic and highlight ones that look promising.
   - Consider your gut reaction (what solution feels intuitively right?) but don't make rash or emotional decisions and watch out for biases.

 CHECK LIST

When evaluating the pros and cons, think through:
- ✓ What is likely to happen if you were to choose each option?
- ✓ What would the worst and best outcomes of making that choice be?
- ✓ How would people react to each option if it were chosen?
- ✓ Which option would resolve the problem long term?
- ✓ Which option is the most realistically attainable, given time, resources and costs?

4. **Select your best option.**
   - Ask the opinion of some relevant people as to which option they would choose.
   - Don't let deliberation become procrastination – make a choice.
   - Once you have decided on an option, let go of the others and move on.

> **TOP TIP**
> KISS (Keep It Simple Stupid!) Try to make the solution as simple as possible. The more complex a solution gets, the harder it is to explain and the easier it is to get wrong.

5. **Make sure the solution can and will happen.**
   - Make the solution attainable. The solution must be real – a theoretical solution is no use. The infrastructure must exist for the solution (you need to work around what you are given).
   - Share the choice with people who will be affected and get their support. People who believe in what they are doing work much harder to make things succeed than people who don't.

6. **Plan the way forward.**
   - Think through and draw up a plan of what will need to be done, by whom and by when.
   - Make sure that the tasks are measurable (mark key milestones) and that the process can be easily checked.
   - Identify possible problems and have a contingency plan that you can put in place if things go wrong.

7. **Get feedback on the plan.**
   - Share the plan with the people who need to implement it and get their support. Adapt the solution if necessary.

8. **Monitor progress.**
   - Check how the plan is going on a regular basis.
   - Make the necessary changes if things are not going according to schedule.

> **TOP TIP**
> Try to understand why things are not working out, don't just keep shifting the deadline. This is valuable information that you can use the next time you have to tackle a problem.

Lessons learned through experience

1. **Understand the problem.**
   - Admit it if you don't understand what exactly you are being asked to solve. Ask questions to clarify the situation and don't accept anything other than clear and distinct ideas.
   - Keep asking questions until you have a clear understanding of what you are meant to do. It is better to understand the problem fully before you start to solve it, rather than pretend you understand and have to come crawling back later when you can't solve the problem.

2. **Manage the deadline.**
   - Break the problem into parts, prioritize them and deliver what you can first. If you try to deliver the whole thing in one go, you may end up delivering nothing for ages and your boss will not be impressed. Deliver, deliver, deliver is the quickest way to getting a job done.

CHECK LIST

When the problem lands on your desk, ask:
- ✓ What do I need to know to solve this?
- ✓ Whom can I talk to?
- ✓ What other resources are available to me?
- ✓ When does it need to be done?
- ✓ Who needs to be told the answer when it is solved?

3. **Get in the right state of mind.**
   - Find a quiet corner or an empty office and block everything else out. You need a clear head to think properly.

4. **Have patience with the problem.**
   - Don't give up if you can't solve the problem in the first 5 minutes.

TOP TIP
Manage your boss's expectations by alerting him/her immediately if you are having problems meeting the deadline.

   - Take a break (e.g. go for a walk or grab a coffee) if you are hitting a brick wall. A change of scenery is usually all that is needed to get the creative juices flowing again.

TOP TIP
If at first you don't succeed, take a break!

5. **Don't be overwhelmed.**
   - Never forget that you can always do something.

 CHECK LIST

Start somewhere:
✓ Put all the concrete information you have down on paper.
✓ Draw a diagram/picture of the problem. Visualization often makes problems easier to understand.
✓ Break up the problem into smaller parts.
✓ Use some problem-solving techniques (see next section).

6. **Don't reinvent the wheel.**
   - Learn from the experiences of previous problems, be they ones you have solved personally or ones solved by someone else. It is usually quicker to find an answer that already exists than to create a new one.

7. **A problem shared is a problem solved.**
   - Never forget that you can easily be biased or blinkered, so ask as many people as you can (within reason) for their ideas. The more options you have, the better choice you can make.
   - Some of the most valuable conversations result from random encounters (e.g. in corridors, on the way to lunch). You can gain a lot just by wandering around and talking to people. Always keep in touch with what everyone is doing.

 TOP TIP
Bounce ideas off people. When you think you have a good idea or a potential answer, do a 'reality check' by asking someone what they think.

8. **Be flexible.**
   - After working on a problem, you may realize that there is something else underlying it that is more important. Accept this new problem and start again.

Tried and trusted techniques

Brainstorming

Brainstorming is a great way to generate lots of ideas in a short amount of time. Its success rests on everyone getting involved and letting their imagination flow. People can be as creative as they want, as all judgement is suspended until the end when the group tries to structure the ideas generated into a set of options.

Steps

1. Gather a group of 5–10 people in a room.
2. Explain what you are there to discuss and give a brief background.
3. Go around the room and get people to give their ideas.
   - Don't be systematic about people speaking, but do get everyone to join in.
   - Make sure everyone understands each point that has been made.
4. Get a scribe to note all the points on a flip chart.
   - Hang the sheets up on the walls for everyone to see.
5. Work through the notes when the group has finished coming up with ideas.
   - Combine similar ideas and discard ones that are irrelevant.

Tips

Know what you want to achieve

TOP TIP
Let the ideas flow naturally.

- Set your goal at the beginning (decide how many ideas you want).

Don't do it in a vacuum

- It works best if people know what they will discuss and have access to some background information prior to the session. If possible, create a fact pack and distribute it 2 days before the session.

Encourage creativity and suspend judgement

- Start with a clean slate.
- Invite lots of suggestions.
- Get everyone to participate.

Put the session's objective before your personal feelings

- Be prepared to have your ideas culled at the end.
- Seek to combine and improve ideas.

Don't let time ruin a good session

- Give yourself enough time but set a time limit of 1–2 hours.
- Give a 5-minute warning before the end of the session.
- Stop at the designated time, unless there is a natural end beforehand.

De Bono's Six Hats

De Bono's Hats is a great way to get people to think differently about the same issue. Each of the six hats represents a different attitude or way of

TOP TIP
Actually having physical hats at the meeting may help the group get involved.

thinking. This is a particularly useful method when you are evaluating the pros and cons of each option. The order in which you wear these hats is entirely up to you and the group. However, it can be helpful to use the hats in a particular sequence.

When wearing:

TOP TIP
Try to avoid over-using the Black Hat.

1. *The White Hat:* **Look at the facts.**
   - Look only at facts and figures. Think about the information you have and the information you need to make a sound decision.

2. *The Red Hat:* **Consider how you feel.**
   - Don't worry about the facts; think about how you feel about each option. What is your gut reaction to each?

3. *The Green Hat:* **Be creative in your thinking.**
   - Think laterally and creatively about each option. Don't be rigid about what's out there already; open your mind to new ideas.

4. *The Blue Hat:* **Look at the big picture.**
   - Stand back and consider each option in the light of the overall situation. Think about what further thinking and work is required on each option.

5. *The Black Hat:* **Outline what is negative.**
   - Think through what the downsides of each option are. What, in your opinion, won't work.

6. *The Yellow Hat:* **Outline what is positive.**
   - Think through what the benefits of each option are.

The Six Hats method was designed by Edward de Bono and is now widely in use. To make full use of this powerful method proper training is advised (contact The Holst Group, e-mail: holstgp@msn.com). The method is mentioned here with permission and may not be reproduced without permission.

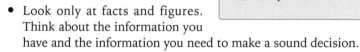
TOP TIP
Most people have a natural tendency to wear one of the hats, so try to encourage everyone to wear all six hats for each item discussed.

6

Research

➡ The research process

➡ Sources of data

➡ Survey techniques

Market and customer knowledge are at the heart of successful business and research is the key to enhancing this knowledge bank of an organization. At some point you will be expected to do research whether it is your field or not. Knowing how to go about it properly is the difference between producing an impressive and informative piece of research and staring at a blank page. This chapter will take you through the research process, show you where to look for data and give you tips for running focus groups, creating questionnaires and getting the most out of interviews.

The research process

1. **Decide your objective.**
    - Be very clear about what your objective (what you are trying to prove) is.
    - Write it down and break it into topics or key underlying ideas.
    - List all the things that you are trying to prove and then list the facts that might help you prove them.

 CHECK LIST

Before doing anything, know:
- ✓ Exactly what you have to research.
- ✓ The output required.
    - Who is the audience?
    - What is the format?
    - When does it need to be done?
- ✓ The resources available.
    - What people and data are available?
- ✓ The deadline.

TOP TIP
Never lose sight of your objective. Don't get hung up on finding a particular fact or a great article that you can remember reading somewhere. Give yourself a time limit to find things and if you can't, move on. Remember, there is more than one way to prove something.

2. **Create a work plan and delegate work if necessary.**
    - List the information that you need and group it into pieces of work that require the same data sources.
    - Delegate each piece of work (if you have the resource) and note who is responsible for completing each one.
    - Draw up a timetable with key milestones and due dates for each piece of work.

TOP TIP
You can often save a lot of time and effort by calling someone who might be able to help you. Remember that people are rarely objective so you must find out or at least double-check important facts yourself. If you do plan to call someone, and have to work late, don't lose track of time; make sure you call before *their* working day is over.

3. **Choose your sources.**
   - Choose sources of data that give you the most accurate detail and are most relevant to your work (e.g. do you need academic literature or the popular press, current or retrospective information, print, sound recordings, images or videos?)
   - Compare how much time and money each source requires.
   - Don't keep using the same sources. Let the information you need dictate what source you should use.

TOP TIP
Note down where you find all information in a logbook. Do this, even if you are not sure you will use it as it will be extremely difficult and time-consuming to get the information later.

4. **Evaluate the information.**
   - How authoritative is the author? Is he/she qualified to write on this subject?
   - How objective is the author? Does he/she appear to be biased or have reason to favour certain things?
   - How accurate is the information? Does it appear to be well researched and easily verifiable?
   - How relevant is the information? Is it up to date?

TOP TIP
Never use information that you can't defend or for which you cannot provide a source.

5. **Check the breadth and depth of your information.**
   - Make sure you have answered all the questions you need to.
   - Make sure that you have sources with different points of view.
   - Decide if getting more information will make a big difference to your work. (Will another article, chart or quote make your work outstanding?)
   - Be very careful if you need to make an assumption. Don't assume to know more than you do and never treat an assumption or estimate as a fact.

6. **Organize and structure your research.**
   - Logically order the information.
   - Decide which format best suits your message and material for communication.
   - Include your sources (all information should be verifiable).
   - Structure the information according to the required format (e.g. proposal, report, email, presentation).

Sources of data

Where possible, get both primary (raw data) and secondary sources (based on primary data). The following sources can be used to find all types of information:

People

- In-house research department
- Company contacts
- Colleagues who have done similar projects.

TOP TIP
Be very clear and specific about what you want when dealing with your in-house research department.

Organizations

- Board of Trade
- Financial institutions (e.g. The World Bank)
- Government departments/Embassies
- PR agencies.

Printed information

- Newspapers (e.g. *Financial Times, The Wall Street Journal*)
- Business magazines run articles on companies and business trends (e.g. *Harvard Business Review, The Economist, Business Week*)
- Marketing magazines give details of successful ad campaigns and website hits (e.g. *Marketing, Marketing Week, New Age Media*)
- Specialist topic magazines may be useful if you are researching a particular area (e.g. pharmaceuticals, music, electricity, finance)
- Bibliographies often provide a valuable source of books and articles on a particular topic
- Yearbooks and directories
- Periodicals
- Books.

Reports and surveys

- Company Annual Report (can be obtained by ringing a company and asking for a copy to be sent to you or by downloading it from the company's website)
- Brokers' reports and investment bank research (copies of these reports can be obtained by contacting the large investment banks)
- The Economist Intelligence Unit (EIU) creates a lot of useful reports.

Internet

(See next section.)

The World Wide Web

There are many free search services on the net. All you have to do is type in the key-word or topic you want to research. The two basic formats are:

- *Internet directories*, which work like library catalogues, compiled by humans.
- *Search engines*, which trawl the web for the best pages on your chosen topic. They give a greater volume of data, but the data may be less accurate.

AltaVista, Excite, Google, Hotbot, InfoSeek, Lycos and Yahoo are some of the most popular search engines. The URL is www before the name and .com or .co.uk (for specific UK searches) after the name.

Internet time savers

Use the Internet at strategic times

- The Internet is quicker when fewer people are online. (European users should use it in the morning when the US is still asleep.)

Be disciplined

- Bookmark a page that interests you but is not related to your research topic. You can look at it later. To bookmark something click 'Add to Bookmarks' (Netscape) or 'Add to Favourites' (Microsoft Explorer).

Be accurate

- Choose words that specifically relate to your topic but are not too broad.
- Use a second term to help narrow the search to make it more relevant.
- Put words in inverted commas if you want them treated as a single entry.
- Double-check that your spelling is correct.

Print out the information

- Print-outs are easier to read than on-screen.

TOP TIP
Learn to speed read. Focus your eyes on the centre of a page and scan the whole sentence in one go, rather than moving your eyes from one side of the line to the other.

Scanning text

Reading magazines, reports and books is an extremely time-consuming way of looking for data. It is much more effective to scan documents for relevant information. To scan a book:

- Look at the content page.
- Read each chapter by looking at the headings only.
- Read the paragraphs by focusing your mind and eye on picking out key words and phrases. Learn to ignore all the small words like 'of', 'at' and 'if'.

Survey techniques

Focus groups

A focus group is a great way to collect qualitative information on a wide variety of topics in a short amount of time. The information generated is not statistically valid or necessarily representative of a population, but it is valuable as a sounding board for ideas. The focus group is made up of a team of people who are brought together to discuss various topics, under the direction of a facilitator.

Roles

Facilitator

- Must know exactly what needs to be achieved before the session starts.
- Asks questions and focuses the discussion on particular topics.
- May be involved in the research or a professional brought in for the job.

Scribe

- Records all the ideas generated.

TOP TIP
The focus group will only be as good as the people involved, so everyone should have a clear understanding of what their role is.

Participants

- Give opinions on the issues raised. (Participants are the only people who should express their opinions.)
- They should be chosen because of their knowledge and relevance to what is being researched.
- There should be no more than 10 people.
- They should sit in a semicircle, all facing the facilitator.

Audience

- There are often other people present who sit in the background and observe the group interaction and listen to what is said.
- It is better if there is no audience as it can make the participants self-conscious.

Steps

1. Decide what you want to research. Set out topics and specific questions.
2. Decide the criteria for the participants.
3. Do a mock focus group with colleagues and refine the approach.
4. Hold the focus group meetings in a comfortable, setting.
5. Collect the notes from the scribe.
6. Analyze the findings.
7. Write up a summary of the findings.

Questionnaires

Questionnaires are an inexpensive way of gathering information on specific questions from a lot of people.

Steps

1. **Decide what you want to learn.**
   - Be very specific about what you want to know.

2. **Decide to whom you should send the questionnaire.**
   - Choose wisely; if you don't question the right people, your research will not be optimal.
   - The size of your sample will depend on your budget, time available and level of relevance to people. It can help to have quotas so that the sample accurately reflects your target population.

3. **Decide what format you will use to ask your questions.**
   - Choose the method (post, web, phone) most appropriate to your budget, time and the sensitivity of the questions.

4. **Decide what questions you want to ask.**
   - Make sure your questions get all the information you need.
   - Decide how you should sequence the questions.

5. **Decide how you are going to collate the information.**
   - Remember that open-ended questions are very hard to summarize, so keep them to a minimum.

6. **Pre-test the questionnaire.**
   - Ask some colleagues for feedback on it.
   - Refine the questionnaire based on the feedback.

7. **Send out the questionnaires/start the phone surveys.**

8. **Collate the data and analyze it.**
   - Keep in mind what you want to learn from the questionnaire and how you will act on the information.

9. **Write up a summary of the results.**

Tips for creating successful questionnaires

Design the questionnaire to suit the format (paper, electronic, phone)

Remember that people will respond to the same question (especially a sensitive one) in different ways depending on how they are asked it

Make sure the questions produce the data required

- Know what you want to learn when devising the questions, and think about how you can collate and use the replies.
- Avoid leading questions (e.g. write 'With which do you agree...?' rather than 'Do you agree with...?').
- Consider the effect that providing something as an option in one question will have on later responses.
- Leave space at the end of the questionnaire for 'Other comments', you never know what nuggets of information you will get.

> **TOP TIP**
> Vary the question type so that you prevent people from giving the same answer to each question (especially when the question is ranked).

Make questions easy to understand

- Use simple words and avoid acronyms and technical terms. If you must use them, explain them the first time they are used.
- Try to write questions that are not left open to interpretation. Make it clear what they mean.
- Never combine two questions into one.
- Don't use double negatives; they are too confusing.

Make sure the question order flows

- Start with general questions and save difficult ones for later.
- Keep similar questions together.
- Number each question.

Make questions easy to answer

- Keep open-ended questions (i.e. open for the respondent to write their answer) to a minimum. Instead, use closed questions (where the respondent must select their answer from a list provided, e.g. multiple choice and yes/no).
- Make sure you leave enough space for the answer of open-ended questions (3–5 lines is a good rule of thumb).
- Avoid difficult recall questions.

CHECK LIST

When creating scales and categories:

✓ Keep the scale simple.
  - Too nuanced (15 different options) a scale may become too subtle or too time-consuming for your audience to answer.
  - Use the same scale throughout the questionnaire.
✓ Make sure the meaning of the scale is clear.
  - Is 1 the lowest or highest score?
✓ Present choices in a logical way.
  - Use positive choices before negative (agree–disagree, yes/no, excellent to poor).
  - Use the higher number on numeric scales to indicate being more in agreement with the question.
  - Be aware that using odd-numbered scales may invite people to keep choosing the middle figure.
✓ Keep your choices unbiased.
  - Try to avoid calling any choices you give 'A' and 'B'. Use neutral letters like 'M' and 'N'.
✓ Cover all possible choices (within reason).
  - Allow 'Don't know', 'Not Applicable', 'Other' or 'None' responses to all questions where that could be a possible valid response. It is possible that people won't know what they think about some things.

Tips for improving response

- Make it as easy as possible to fill out (check boxes or circle responses).
- Ask questions in the third person, it is less threatening.
- Pre-test the survey with 5–10 people before sending it out. Examine the questionnaire for flow and understanding.
- Include a one-page cover memo that answers all the who, why, what, where, when and how questions.
- Include a prepaid, stamped, addressed response envelope.
- Incentivize response. (For those done by email, write something in the message box, e.g. 'Free X', 'Win Y' or 'Please respond by Monday'.)
- End with a thank you and an address indicating where responses should be sent (assume the questionnaire and cover letter will become separated).

TOP TIP
Make the questionnaire short. Only ask what it is essential to know.

Interviewing

There are three steps to interviewing; preparation, conducting and documentation.

Preparing interviews

1. **Choose the interview type (phone, face-to-face).**
   The interview type is determined by:
   - How formal you want it to be.
   - The questions you need to ask.
   - Your interviewees.

2. **Decide on the interviewee.**
   - Decide whom you want to interview and arrange a time for the interview.
   - Find out as much as you can about the person you are interviewing beforehand (e.g. their responsibilities, influence and biases).

> **TOP TIP**
> Find out what is going on in the company and the initiatives taking place in the interviewee's area; you don't want to be perceived as ignorant.

3. **Prepare the questions.**
   - Draft questions that will give you the information you need to make a decision.
   - Group together questions that deal with the same topic.
   - Start with the more familiar and impersonal topics and move towards the more complex and debatable issues as the interview progresses.
   - Think through potential problem areas and plan how to deal with them.

> **TOP TIP**
> Remember that you are constrained by time, so choose your questions carefully and make sure you cover all the important issues before it is too late.

4. **Send a reminder.**
   - Send the person a short email (four working days before the interview) with details of when and where the meeting will take place, who will be present, how long you expect it to last, and the topics you hope to cover.

Conducting interviews

1. **Arrive early.**
   - Give yourself plenty of time to get there.
   - Call if you are going to be late.

2. **Introduce yourself (and others as necessary).**
   - Spend a couple of minutes establishing a rapport.
   - Thank the person for their time.

3. **Introduce the interview.** *Outline:*
   - What the aim of the interview is.
   - How the interview will proceed.
   - What you intend to do with the information.

MIND YOUR MANNERS!

Always send a thank-you note/email after the interview.

4. **Ask the questions.**
   - Keep your language simple.
   - Listen carefully to the replies.

5. **Paraphrase answers.**
   - Make sure that you have understood correctly.

6. **Be conscious of time.**
   - Step up the pace rather than overrun the time scheduled.
   - Make sure you ask the most important questions.

7. **Tie up the loose bits at the end of the meeting.**
   - Sum up the main points and state what the next steps are.
   - Thank the person for their time and information.
   - Ask if you may call with follow-up questions, if necessary.
   - Leave your contact details.

Interview documentation

Record the information
- Note when and where the meeting took place and who was there.
- Record points made and relevant quotations.

Tips for getting the information
- Number your questions and use the numbers for note taking.
- Develop ways of writing quickly but accurately.
- Try to write neatly and legibly and fill in missing data when you can.
- Never put your note pad on the desk; keep it in your lap.
- Write up notes immediately after the interview, when your mind is fresh.

Questioning techniques

Techniques for getting the answers:

- Start with broad questions: ('Tell me about ... '/'Describe ... ') and move towards getting more detail (Who? What? Where? When? How? Be careful about asking Why? as it can be very subjective).

Techniques for getting more information:

- Put the interviewee at ease with gentle, coaxing questions (e.g. 'What about ... ?', 'Would you like to say more about ... ?', 'Is it possible that ... ?', 'Maybe ...'). Be careful not to put words into the interviewee's mouth.

Techniques for keeping the interviewee on track:

- Don't let the interviewee wander off a topic (it happens a lot). A gentle reminder should help (e.g. 'Can we talk about ... ?', 'Would you like to talk about ... now?', 'Can you expand on the point you made earlier?').

Tips for telephone interviews

- Introduce yourself and state the purpose of the call.
- State the expected length of the interview.
- Ask if the person can take the call or if you could call back at a more convenient time.
- Speak clearly and distinctly.
- Sound friendly and trustworthy.
- Avoid long silences. Give verbal clues that you are listening.
- Avoid discussing sensitive.

CHAPTER 7

Financial awareness

⇒ Getting good with numbers

⇒ Budgeting basics

⇒ Principles of spreadsheets

⇒ The Annual Report made easy

⇒ Measuring company performance

Being good with numbers can be an invaluable asset when faced with an impromptu problem in the workplace. Making an effort to improve your numerical skills is worthwhile; people who are numerate are often perceived as people who are smart. Even if you have never been good at maths, don't worry. This chapter shows you how to budget and create impressive spreadsheets. It also takes a practical look at the numerical side of work and provides some basic financial knowledge so you should feel more comfortable when working with numbers in the future.

Getting good with numbers

Even if you are quite good with numbers, you may still encounter difficulties and get stuck on certain things. While the following is not intended as a comprehensive guide, it outlines some of the common areas of confusion and is a good place to start if you want to improve your ability to work with numbers, quickly.

Getting comfortable with numbers

Try to get a feel for the numbers you work with

- It is important to keep a sense of what the significant figures are, especially when doing calculations in your head. Multiplying 7,123,235 by 61 is not easy. However, multiplying 7 million by 60 is not that hard. Round numbers off to make them easier to calculate but develop a feel for what kind of margin of error you are introducing by doing this.

TOP TIP
Do maths problems in your head even if it is only on an approximate basis. It helps to keep you sharp and is a good check on manual errors on calculators.

Round numbers using the accepted rule

- Any decimal that ends in a 4 or less should be rounded off to the lower number (e.g. 2.4 becomes 2.0, not 3.0). Any decimal that ends in a 5 or higher should be rounded off to the higher number (e.g. 2.5 becomes 3.0, not 2.0).
- If the number has many decimal points, keep applying the rule (e.g. 1.90735 = 1.9074 = 1.907 = 1.91 = 1.9 = 2).

Understand notation on calculators

Sometimes calculators can express very small or large numbers by using scientific notation:

$10^6 = 10 \times 10 \times 10 \times 10 \times 10 \times 10 = 1,000,000$ (e.g. $3.45 \times 10^6 = 3,450,000$)

$10^{-6} = 1/10 \times 1/10 \times 1/10 \times 1/10 \times 1/10 \times 1/10 = 0.000001$ (e.g. $3.45 \times 10^{-6} = 0.00000345$)

Don't confuse equalities and inequalities

$>$ means 'is greater than' (e.g. $6 > 4$). The 'mouth' faces the larger number.

$<$ means 'is less than' (e.g. $4 < 6$). The 'mouth' faces the larger number.

$\leq$ means 'is less than or equal to'.

$\neq$ means 'is not equal to'.

$\cong$ means 'is approximately equal to'.

Using algebra

Algebra can be a great way to solve complex problems. Don't worry if you were never good at algebra at school, or can't even remember what it is, because although you do need to know it for business maths, you will only ever have to use the very basics.

Algebra is when you write out a problem, expressing it mathematically (otherwise known as a formula), in order to ascertain what the known numbers are and what you are trying to solve for (e.g. Profit = Revenue *minus* Expenditure). If you know all but one of the variables, you can solve it.

There are certain conventions in algebra that you may want to use if you are sharing your description of the problem with others.

- Lower-case letters at the beginning of the alphabet (e.g. a, b, c) are usually reserved for constants.
- Lower-case letters at the end of the alphabet (e.g. x, y, z) are reserved for variables. x or y are usually reserved for the major unknowns in the equation.
- n expresses the number of observations.
- t is used for time.
- r is usually an interest rate.

Avoiding problems with percentage increases

Don't forget to add/subtract the percentage increase/decrease to the original number to get the new number

- To increase something by a percentage, multiply it by 1 *plus* the percentage increase (e.g. to increase 10 by 8%: $10 \times (1+0.08) = 10 \times (1.08) = 10.8$).
- To decrease by a percentage, multiply the number by 1 *minus* the percentage decrease (e.g. to decrease 10 by 8%: $10 \times (1 - 0.08) = 10 \times (0.92) = 9.2$).

Don't assume that a percentage increase followed by the same percentage decrease arrives back at the original number; it doesn't

- As the initial percentage increase is calculated on a lower number than that on which the second percentage decrease is calculated, it will always arrive at a lower number (e.g. 10 increased by 50% equals 15 but 15 reduced by 50% equals 7.5.)

Don't confuse percentage point moves and percentage changes

- If a percentage increases from 20% to 25% it has gone up five percentage points. However, the percentage increase is 25% $([25 - 20]/20 \times 100) = (5/20 \times 100) = (1/4 \times 100)$. This can lead to confusion so be very clear about which you mean.

Never lose sight of absolute increases

- Always understand the numbers behind a percentage increase it doesn't show.

In Figure 7.1, Japanese operations look as if they are doing well when you look at their profit growth rate. However when you look at the actual profit figures, you see that they are very low (i.e. even though profit grew a lot between 2000 and 2001, it is still much lower than the US and Europe).

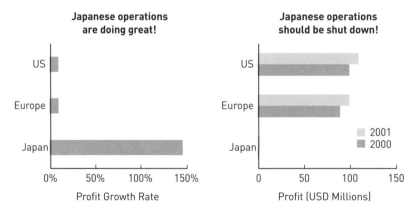

Figure 7.1

Working with fractions, decimals, percentages and ratios

Be able to move easily from fractions and decimals to percentages

- A fraction can be converted into a decimal by dividing the numerator (top) by the denominator (bottom) (e.g. 7/8 = 0.875).
- Multiply a decimal number by 100 to convert it to a percentage (e.g. 0.875 × 100 = 87.5%). Multiplying a decimal by 100 just moves the decimal point two places to the right (one place for each 0).

> **TOP TIP**
> Remember that fractions, decimals and percentages are all different ways of saying the same thing (e.g. 7/8 = 0.875 = 87.5%).

Know where to put the decimal point when multiplying

- Multiplying with decimals can cause problems. The trick is to add the number of places to the right of the decimals in the numbers being multiplied and ensure you have that number of decimal places in your answer (e.g. 1.3 × 1.7 = 2.21).

> **TOP TIP**
> Check you have put the decimal point in the right place by rounding the numbers both up and down and multiplying them (e.g. 1.3 × 1.4, you know that since both are more than 1 and less than 2, your answer has to be somewhere between 1 (1 × 1) and 4 (2 × 2). The answer is 1.82 and you know this is right because 0.182 would be too low and 18.2 too high.

Know how to divide decimals quickly

- Multiply the number you are dividing by, by a multiple of 10 to get rid of the decimal point (e.g. 0.85 would be multiplied by 100 and 0.065 would be multiplied by 1,000). Then multiply the number you are dividing into by the same multiple of 10 as you must multiply both the numerator and denominator by the same number. Once you have done that, divide as normal (e.g. 1.6/0.8 = 16/8 = 2).

Know how to work out ratios

- Ratios are another way to work out how a total amount is divided. To work out the actual shares you need, add the ratios together, divide your answer into the total amount and work out the shares by multiplication (e.g. if you need to divide £100 in the ratio 1:2:2 then 1 + 2 +2 = 5; 100/5 = 20; so 1 × 20 =20 and 2 × 20 = 40; £100 is divided £20: £40: £40).

Calculating averages

Averages are a great way to bring order to a mass of data. In essence they summarize data by identifying the midpoint of a related set of numbers. There are many ways of calculating an average:

Mean

- As a general rule, the mean is probably the most appropriate average, unless there is a good reason for selecting another.
- It is calculated by adding all of the numbers in a dataset and dividing by the number of observations.

   Sample = 1, 2, 2, 2, 3, 3, 4, 5, 6, 6 $\Rightarrow$ mean = 34/10 = 3.4

Median

- The median can be a useful concept as it is less affected by extreme values.
- It is best to use the median if it highlights the point you want to make, or if the data cannot have a mean (e.g. ordinal data).
- It is calculated by taking the *middle* observation in a ranked series.
- If there is an even number of observations the two central values should be added and divided by two.

   Sample = 1, 2, 2, 2, 3, 3, 4, 5, 6, 6 median = 3

Standard deviation

- An average means more when you know what the spread or dispersion (the range of values) is. Standard deviation measures this dispersion.
- Two different data series could have the same mean but vastly different dispersions; one with all the numbers in the series at or close to the mean (e.g. the average salary of a company could be £15,000 with a dispersion of £12,000–£18,000), the other with a number much higher than the mean counterweighted by a number much lower than the mean (e.g. same average salary of £15,000 with a dispersion of £5,000–£150,000).
- It is unlikely that you would want to calculate it by hand (it is very tedious), so use a spreadsheet package like Excel to calculate it for you.

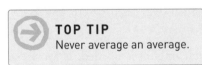

TOP TIP
Never average an average.

Budgeting basics

The word 'budget' often strikes fear into people who see it as something constrain-ing, awkward and time-consuming but a budget helps you track costs against estimates. It is extremely worthwhile knowing how to put a budget together, even if your job is one that does not require regular use of budgets, as it is likely that you will need to create one at some stage in your career.

Creating a budget

1. **Collect the information you need.**

CHECK LIST
Make sure you get:
✓ **A copy of last year's budget.**
  – Find out how, where, when and why money is spent in your department.
  – Try to get a copy that has been updated with what actually happened.
  – Get a copy of the accounts if you can't get a copy of the budget.
✓ **A list of all your expenses and sources of revenue.**
  – Have a chat with your boss to understand the level of detail you are expected to provide.
  – Ask the right people for the information. Be courteous and give them plenty of time. Don't forget that you are asking a favour.
✓ **A list of the risks or factors that will have a constraining effect on your budget.**
  – Remember that these risks may be internal (e.g. limited funds available) or external (e.g. downturn in the marketplace).

2. **Set up categories.**
   - Find out if your company or department has a standard budget template. If there is one, it is best to use it, although you may need to modify it somewhat to meet your needs.

   TOP TIP
   Check all information for accuracy.

   - Avoid blindly copying all the categories from last year's budget. Ask yourself if there are categories that are still relevant or if new categories need to be added.

TOP TIP
You can create a simple but impressive budget on a spreadsheet.

3. **Decide the timeframe.**
   - Find out how your company or department breaks up the financial calendar. Is it monthly (12 months or 13 four-week months), biannually (two periods of six months), quarterly (four periods of three months) or weekly (52 weeks)?
   - Break down the budget into periods of time that mean something and are manageable if there is no standard.

4. **Calculate budget amounts and write in estimates.**
   - Collect bills, receipts, past performance data and anything that will help you make more accurate estimates for the future.
   - Make assumptions (if you can't get good data) using all the information you have collected, including your list of risks and constraining factors. Never base an assumption on another assumption.
   - Go through each item on last year's budget and see if you need to spend more or less this year. Be as realistic as possible.
   - Build in some contingency but don't overbudget; your plan should motivate and inspire you.
   - Find out how your company or department rounds figures. If there is no standard, it is common practice to round pounds to the nearest hundreds (above 50 is 100, below 50 down to the lower hundred, e.g. £66.54 would be £100 and so would £123.46) and hundreds to the nearest thousand in a similar manner (e.g. £668.11 would become £1,000 and £1,481.42 would be £1,000).

> **TOP TIP**
> Take extra care when budgeting for staffing. Staffing costs a lot and tends to make up a big part of any budget. This cost can also change a lot (due to promotions or bonuses), creating havoc with your budget, so make sure you think through what could happen to this figure.

5. **Revise the budget.**
   - Go through each item and realistically assess whether you need that much; people tend to overestimate on the first draft.
   - Show your first draft to your boss and get him/her to suggest areas that could be trimmed. It shouldn't take more than 15 minutes and he/she will usually be happy to do this, as he/she will probably have to provide the funding.

> **TOP TIP**
> Be realistic and only ask for what you need. You should aim to get your budget approved on the first submission.

6. **Check your figures.**

   - Make sure all of your figures are as accurate as possible and that you can explain where you got them (including any assumptions on which they may be based).
   - Check that the totals are correct.
   - Make sure you have the appropriate amount of detail. Cut out things that are insignificant in the grand scheme of things.

TOP TIP
Know what each category in the budget costs as a percentage of the total budget.

7. **Create a professional-looking document.**

   - Put a cover page with your name, the name of your department and the name of the budget (e.g. Marketing Budget 2002).
   - Make the budget one page only (landscape format).
   - Include a page of notes that explain anything that may be unclear.

8. **Submit your budget for approval.**

   - Think about how you are going to convince your boss to give you the amount you want, as he/she will want to keep expenditure to a minimum.
   - Negotiate for time and resources as well as money.
   - Put all your source data in easy-to-read notes in case you are asked to explain where you got your numbers.
   - Make sure you understand why it wasn't approved (if it is rejected) and make the necessary changes to ensure approval the next time.

9. **Maintain the budget.**

   - Fill in actual figures as and when they occur.
   - Look at the difference between the actual budget and estimated budget and understand why there is a difference. Revise the numbers upward or downward as necessary.
   - Don't worry if there are variances (difference between the actual figure and the budgeted figure), as there always will be. Just decide how best to deal with them (e.g. do you need to revise the budget or take corrective steps in your work?).

TOP TIP
Stay on top of your budget; it will help you monitor performance and make you look good during budget reviews.

2002 Budget (£'000s)	Jan			Feb			Mar			Apr			May			Jun			Total		
	Est	Act	Var	Est	Act	Var	Est	Act	Var	Est	Act	Var	Est	Act	Var	Est	Act	Var	Est	Act	Var
Revenue																					
Sales of Service A																					
Sales of Service B																					
Sales of Service C																					
Total Rev/Exp																					
Expenses *Fixed Costs*																					
Rent																					
Taxes																					
Other Overheads																					
Variable Costs																					
Staffing																					
Training																					
Entertainment																					
Office Admin																					
Travel																					
Total Expenses																					

Figure 7.2 Sample semi-annual budget

Definitions:

➡ Est = Estimate budget figure.

➡ Act = Actual figure.

➡ Var = Variance (Estimate *less* Actual).

➡ Revenue or Allocated Expenditure = Money in. Your money comes either from revenue you generate from sales or money you are allocated.

➡ Expenses = Money out. The bills you have to pay.

➡ Fixed Costs = Costs that stay the same irrespective of scale of operations. Someone senior in the organization sets fixed costs.

➡ Variable Costs = Costs that are directly linked to the scale of operations. You have some control over the variable costs so you should focus your attention on them.

 TOP-TIP
Total things downward by month and across by item to check if you get the same number.

Tips for creating budgets

Keep them simple

- Be ruthless about the number of categories; confine it to the major revenue and expense headings.

Make your numbers as accurate as possible

- Check, check and re-check your numbers. One little mistake could throw the whole thing.
- Ask a colleague to look through it if it is an extremely important budget. It is easy to make a mistake when you are dealing with so many numbers.

Make sure they are complete

- Think through everything that people would need to know from your budget and check that you have left nothing important out.

Make sure they are compatible with other budgets

- Check out the standard budgets your company uses, especially if you have to submit your budget to a committee or if it has to feed into a departmental budget.
- Make sure it looks similar to other budgets (if there is no company standard), by using a similar typeface, page size and layout.

Make them attractive and easy to understand

- Make it visually appealing but don't go overboard on the use of colour and unusual typefaces. The document should retain a certain gravitas.
- Ask a colleague's opinion; what is obvious to you may not be to others.

TOP TIP
A well-presented budget instils confidence and is more likely to be approved.

CHECK LIST
Examples of effective formatting:
- ✓ Put the categories in logical order.
- ✓ Be consistent with numbers (e.g. use the same number of decimal places).
- ✓ Space everything out.
- ✓ Use language that is concise and appropriate.
- ✓ Try to highlight the numbers that are most important.
- ✓ Keep notes brief and put them on a separate page.

Principles of spreadsheets

Spreadsheets are a fantastic tool that can make numerical problems a lot easier to work out. Even if you don't consider yourself good at maths, or you don't need to use them very often, you should spend some time getting good at them.

Buy a book

- If you are prepared to invest some time in getting better, there are a multitude of books on the market that will cater to your level.

Ask a colleague

- By far the best and quickest way to improve is to find a colleague who is a 'spreadsheeting genius' and ask whether he/she can teach you a few things. It is amazing what you can pick up in a few minutes.

Experiment

- Another great way is to look at the different options open to you and see what happens when you use them. When you start to feel comfortable with your spreadsheet package, you will get a feel for the way the program operates. You can always use the help function if you get stuck.

Financial models

Creating a model is not hard, but creating an excellent model does require application and practice. The following tips should prove useful:

1. **Think through what you want from the model.**
   - Ask yourself what the problem you are trying to solve is and what decisions will be taken based on the models output.

2. **Work it out on paper.**
   - Spend time thinking through what your model may have to do. Although a model tends to evolve over time, you will make life a lot easier if you think through the kind of things you may have to add on at a later stage and allow for them from the beginning.
   - Draw the model out on various pages before you begin.

3. **Build it from the bottom up.**
   - Enter any raw data that you will need.
   - Make your best guess for the data that you don't have, as it is unlikely you will have all the information you need. Record the fact that it is a guess and update it as soon as the information becomes available.
   - Build up the model over a number of worksheets if necessary. You can link the sheets together by using formulae to pick up data on other sheets.

Spreadsheet tips

Keep saving

- Get into the habit of saving regularly (at least every 10 minutes). It may seem like an effort, but the risk of losing hours, even days of work should be enough to justify it.
- Make back-up copies of your work as well.

MORE INFO?

See p. 28 for more on saving data.

TOP TIP

Never hardcode (type in) numbers in formulae or re-input numbers that are already on other sheets.

Ensure your numbers are accurate

- Build self-checks into your models as it is very easy to make mistakes when you have to build complex models (especially if you end up working on them for long periods of time, or late at night).

Make your spreadsheet easy to understand

- Create a logical structure that is simple to follow.
- Title and date all sheets and label cells.
- State what units were used (e.g. £'000 is used for thousands of pounds; £m for millions of pounds).
- Explain all calculations and assumptions by either having a separate assumption page or by inserting a comment in the actual cell.

Make your spreadsheet clean and readable

- Try to fit each section of analysis to one page.
- Rename the worksheets to make them easy to follow.
- Experiment to see what style you like, but try to keep things relatively conservative.
- Don't underestimate the appearance of the model.

CHECK LIST

Examples of effective formatting:

- ✓ Remove the gridlines and leave the background white.
- ✓ Use black font for hard-coded data and blue for derived data.
- ✓ Consistently format numbers to one or two decimal places (e.g. 7.0) and use commas to denote breaks (e.g. 1,000).
- ✓ Change the width of the column to fit the contents.
- ✓ Highlight cells that are of particular interest (e.g. titles and totals) by changing the colour of the cell, making them bold or italic or by putting a border around the cell.
- ✓ Align the text with the numbers or centre it.

The Annual Report made easy

Even if you work in an area that involves no finance or accounting whatsoever, it is worthwhile spending a few minutes becoming familiar with your company's Annual Report. It is an invaluable source of information that will help you understand the direction in which your company is heading and its financial health. There are so many things that could be said about the Annual Report and the financial statements that make it up, but as the aim of this book is to cover the essentials bear the following in mind:

– The Annual Report is made up of a series of written statements (mission statements that outline the company's vision and strategy, the Chairman's statement and reports of the Chief Executive and Directors) and financial statements (balance sheet, cash flow, income statement). Together they show the past year's performance and outline plans for the coming year.

– Financial accounts must be prepared annually by every commercial business (in which the public has been invited to become involved) in order to agree a tax liability and to provide those interested in its activities (e.g. shareholders, lenders, employees) with appropriate information and the ability to assess the adequacy of management of the organization's operations and assets.

– Drawing up the accounts is governed by strict legal requirements and informal guidelines created by the accounting profession. However, no two sets of accounts will be the same, as different businesses operate in different ways and use different accounting policies.

– Companies will tend to disclose minimal information and although everything they show will be true, it will be presented in its most acceptable form; the Annual Report is also used as an advertising document.

– The Company Directors produce the set of accounts that they present to shareholders at the Annual General Meeting (AGM) but the shareholders appoint auditors to check the accounts. The auditors are accountants independent of the management of the company who make sure that the published accounts give a true and fair view of the company's performance, and stick to established conventions.

The financial statements

Profit and Loss Account/Income Statement

This statement shows how the company has been doing over the past year. It shows the company's revenue and then takes away all the expenses (items that went into creating that revenue) to show whether the company made a profit or loss for that year. Starting with revenue, expenses are subtracted in a particular order. As they are taken away, they show various levels of profit. Some of the most useful are:

- Gross profit (sales less cost of sales). This is an important figure and one watched carefully by management and investors
- Operating profit (gross profit less all the expenses supporting the infrastructure and administration of an organization, e.g. rent and salaries)
- Profit before tax (operating profit less interest incurred on borrowings for the year, plus interest received)
- Profit after tax (profit before tax less the tax due as a result of trading for the year)
- Retained profit (profit after tax less any dividend paid to the shareholders. This money is ploughed back into the business).

Cash Flow Statement

This statement shows how well the company manages its use of cash. It follows a standard format and is sectioned into meaningful blocks of subtotals, providing clear information on the cash movements within an organization's key activities.

- Operating cash flow (operating profit from the P&L adjusted for non-cash items, e.g. depreciation)
- Cash flow before financing (operating cash flow less non-trading items, e.g. interest, dividends, tax and capital expenditure)
- Movement in cash (operating cash flow before financing plus financing, e.g. loans and share capital). This is the bottom line of the cash flow and shows the increase or decrease in cash in the period.

> **TOP TIP**
> Although the Profit and Loss and Balance Sheet are often considered more important, attention should be paid to the Cash Flow Statement. It is possible that a company could be profitable but have severe cash flow difficulties and without cash a business can die. Never confuse profit with cash; cash pays bills, profit doesn't.

Balance Sheet

This statement shows everything that the company owns (its assets) and how it paid for them (liabilities and equity) on a particular date (usually the end of the reporting period). It is called a balance sheet because the cost of the assets should balance or equal the amount paid for them (liabilities and equity). Thus the basic equation of the balance sheet is Assets = Liabilities + Equity. The statement is split into sections according to strict accounting rules:

Assets

– Fixed assets (assets used by the business for the business, e.g. equipment or the company's brand name).
– Current assets (short-term assets, if not already in cash form will be converted into cash within the next 12 months, e.g. stock, debtors/people who owe you money).

Liabilities

– Long-term liabilities (debts due beyond the next 12 months, e.g. long-term debts and loans).
– Current liabilities (debts due in the next 12 months, e.g. creditors/people you owe money and bank overdrafts).

  (*Note:* Working capital, also known as net current assets (current assets *less* current liabilities) is an important figure. A company does not want what it owes in the next 12 months (current liabilities) to exceed what it has coming in (current assets) as this is a recipe for insolvency.)

Equity/shareholder funds

– The investment that shareholders put in a company. It is a form of long-term finance. Equity also includes any retained profit that is ploughed back into the business.

CHECK LIST

Accounting terms often vary from country to country.
✓ Trade debtors = accounts receivable
✓ Trade creditors = accounts payable
✓ Stock = inventory

TOP TIP

You should not see the balance sheet as an indication of the company's worth as all the items are shown at the price paid for them (historical cost) and not at their current market value.

Measuring company performance

There are many ways to measure the performance of a company and with a little time and effort, you can get a good understanding of what a company's strategy and financial position are. Some basic analysis and regular reading of a business news-paper like the *Wall Street Journal* or the *Financial Times* is a good place to start.

Financial ratio analysis

Financial ratio analysis is a useful way of putting a company's annual accounts into perspective. It allows an analysis of a company's performance through time, facilitates cross-company analysis, and forms a template for the key questions to ask about a business. Be careful though: industry sectors, company size and business mix all affect a company's figures, so make sure you compare like with like. The four main types of ratio are liquidity ratios, profitability ratios, activity ratios and leverage ratios.

Guidelines for successful financial analysis

Keep it simple

- Don't make things too complicated as you will lose sight of what you are trying to show.

Do your own analysis

- Never rely on someone else's analysis – most annual reports provide financial highlights that are interesting but carefully picked.
- Base the company assessment and calculations on the original financial data avail-able in the financial statements.
- Take five companies (in the same sector) and build an industry average. Compare the company you are interested in against that average.

Look for a trend or comparison

- Compare this year's ratio with that of the previous year to see how it changed. Ideally 3–5 years' figures should be analyzed in order to get a clear view of the consistency of a company's performance and to highlight any movements in the ratios that require explanation or investigation.
- Compare the ratio of one company with that of another operating in the same business and of comparable size (i.e. compare like with like).

Get behind the figures

- Understand the reasons behind a large move in a particular entry or ratio. While the financial statements are important in assessing a company, you should also look at its strategy and competitive position in the industry.

Read the notes to the accounts

- Make sure that consistent figures are used in ratios being developed. Companies may change the way in which they define individual items in the financial state-ments or there may be other anomalies highlighted in the notes.

Liquidity ratios

Liquidity ratios measure the company's ability to meet its financial obligations. A company is said to be 'liquid' if it can turn its assets into cash quickly. Current assets (e.g. debtors, inventory or stock) are assets that are due to be turned into cash within a year.

To measure how easily a company can pay its bills:

- Current Ratio = Current Assets *divided by* Current Liabilities
- Acid Test Ratio = (Current Assets *less* Inventory) *divided by* Current Liabilities.

The Acid Test Ratio does not include inventory because when a firm gets into difficulties, it is not always easy to quickly liquidate assets at the price held on the balance sheet.

Note: Normally it is expected that a company should have at least as many current assets as current liabilities.

Profitability ratios

These ratios attempt to measure the profitability of a company in relation to different aspects of the business.

To measure how much profit is being generated in relation to long-term capital invested:

- Return on Capital Employed (RoCE) = Profit before interest and taxes *divided by* (Long-term liabilities *plus* Share capital). This is a key ratio.

Note: People put money into companies to make a return and if this return is not good, they might choose to invest their money elsewhere.

To measure how much profit is being generated in relation to the assets employed:

- Operating profit as a percentage of total assets = Profit before interest and taxes *divided by* Total Assets (= PBIT/TA).

Note: The income statement might be very impressive but due to the fact that there are a lot of assets behind it.

To measure how efficient the company is at minimizing costs while maximizing revenue:

- Profit as a percentage of sales = Net Profit after taxes *divided by* Net Sales (= PAT/Sales).

To measure how profitably the company is utilizing the shareholders' funds:

- Return on equity % = Profit after tax, minority and preference dividends *divided by* Ordinary Share Capital and Reserves.

To measure the return on capital for a specific period:

- Earnings per share = Profit after tax, minority interests and preference dividends *divided by* Weighted Average Number of Ordinary Shares.

Note: Dividends are a cash payment to equity holders and are decided by directors. They don't measure how much could have been paid to shareholders.

Activity ratios

Activity ratios indicate how well a company is using its assets.

From a fixed asset perspective:

– Poor activity ratios may indicate that obsolete plant, equipment or manufacturing techniques are being employed.

From a current asset perspective:

– Inventory not being sold quickly enough could indicate flawed distribution channels, a highly competitive market or simply a product that is not in demand.

– An increase in the average sales collection period could indicate that the company needs to grant more and more credit to shift inventory, that this side of the business is being mismanaged or that there is a credit problem on the purchasing side.

To measure the amount of assets needed to generate sales:

– Total asset turnover = Sales *divided by* Total Assets.

Note: The sales and profit numbers for a company may be impressive but if a company requires an enormous amount of assets to generate these sales, the business may not have a long-term future.

To measure how quickly stock is sold:

– Inventory days = Stock *divided by* Average Inventory Sales per day where Average Inventory Sales per day = Cost of Goods Sold *divided by* 365.

Note: The quicker stock is sold, the healthier the company probably is.

To measure how long debtors are taking to pay for sales:

– Trade Debtor Days = Trade Debtors *divided by* Average Sales per day where Average Sales per day = Sales *divided by* 365.

Note: An increase in this number can indicate problems on the demand side.

> **TOP TIP**
> Try to find out what a good or bad number might be for each of these ratios for your industry as what is acceptable for one industry may be worrying for another.

Leverage ratios

Leverage ratios indicate how a company is financed in terms of debt versus equity. The balance between debt and equity is a key indicator of a company's financial health. Too much debt and a company is 'highly geared'. Leverage (a lot of debt) can increase the return on equity but it also increases the riskiness of the business due to the obligation to make interest payments on the debt.

To measure how much debt the company has undertaken:

– Gearing or leverage ratio = Total Debt (long term and short term) *divided by* equity. This is a key ratio.

To measure the ability of a company to meet its interest payments:

– Interest Cover (times) = Profit before interest and tax (PBIT) *divided by* interest expense.

To measure the average number of days that the company is taking to pay its suppliers:

– Days Payable = Trade Creditors *divided by* average Purchases per day (where Average Purchases per day ≅ Cost of Goods sold *divided by* 365 days). Cost of Goods sold is used as a proxy for purchases from suppliers, although it actually includes other costs such as labour.

 CHECK LIST How much debt versus equity should a firm or project have?

Look at the company's:

✓ **Business risk**

– If a company has a lot of business risk then it may not make sense to borrow a lot. It can be a lethal cocktail for a company to have high business risk and high financial risk. A firm that has a safe and consistent set of cash flows year in year out is in a position to take on debt more comfortably.

✓ **Tax position**

– Interest is paid prior to taxation (whereas equity dividends are not), so interest payments on debt can reduce a company's tax liability. If a company views its tax bill as likely to be consistent in the future, it may make sense to take on more debt.

✓ **Asset composition**

– Where a business has saleable tangible assets, it can sell these if it gets in distress. However, if a company has more intangible assets, it is less likely to have this sale option at its disposal. Lenders will lend more to companies who can pledge tangible assets against their borrowings.

✓ **Flexibility**

– Not having too much debt means that if the need arises it will be easier to borrow money quickly at attractive levels.

Financial newspapers

It is important to read the financial press to know about particular firms, sectors and markets that impact on your job and company. Even if you don't read every page of the financial newspapers, it is useful to read the front page and the main editorial section, as these will give you a flavour of the main topics of the day. You can then quickly scan the rest of the paper for topics that are of particular interest to you. The following section will help you to interpret the more important technical information and topics you will encounter.

- Stock market indices
- Individual stocks
- Interest rates
- Foreign exchange
- Other economic indicators.

Stock market indices

When people refer to the stock market going up or down, they mean that a particular stock market *index* has gone up or down. The index is made up of shares (selected by the particular exchange) and weights the price movement of each share by the value of the company (market capitalization) to calculate an index movement. Therefore, the share price movement of a larger company will have a greater effect on the index than the same movement on the share price of a smaller company. Some individual stocks may have gone up in price and some may have gone down, but it is important to know what the overall market has done. It is the change of value of the index over time that is important rather than the absolute value. The major stock market indices are:

- Dow Jones Industrial Average (a US index of the 30 largest companies)
- Standard and Poor's 500 (a US index containing a broad group of companies)
- Nasdaq (a US index of technology-related stocks)
- FTSE 100 (an index of the 100 largest companies in the UK)
- Nikkei (the major Japanese stock market index).

When looking at indices, the important information to monitor is:

- *(YTD) Year to date percentage change:* The amount an index has gone up or down since 1 January.
- *Close/last price:* The official value of the index at the close of trading.
- *Previous:* The value of the index at the close of business the previous day.
- *Percentage change:* The percentage change of the index over the trading day.

Individual stocks

Individual stocks are normally listed in newspapers and are grouped in terms of industry sectors. All prices are expressed in the local currency of the exchange using the smallest denomination possible (i.e. UK shares will be in pence and US shares will be in cents). Individual stock prices will be published in a format that can be confusing the first time you see it, but which is actually quite simple.

52 week							Vol	
High	Low	Stock	Dividend	Yield	PE	Close	000's	Net Change
300	200	Imaginary Corp.	10	4	15	250	250	10

While the format may vary slightly between newspapers, the following should enable you to interpret the various different headings:

- *52 week high and low:* This is the highest and lowest price of the stock in the last year.
- *Stock:* This is the name of the company trading its shares (stock = shares).
- *Dividend:* The last dividend paid to shareholders. Companies decide how much to pay, although they are not obliged to pay anything.
- *Yield:* The dividend return you could expect if you bought the shares at today's price. It is the last dividend paid, expressed as a percentage of the current share price. It should be noted that there is no guarantee that the company will pay the same dividend next year; a lot of shares are bought for their potential price appreciation rather than dividend payments.
- *Close/last/price:* The last price at which the stock traded (technically it may not actually be the last price but rather an average of the last few trading prices).
- *PE:* The Price/Earnings ratio expresses the value of a company in terms of the amount of profit it generates. It is calculated by dividing the current share price by the published earnings per share for the previous year.
- *High and low price (not shown):* The highest and lowest price of the stock during the day's trading. It gives an idea of how volatile the stock was on that particular day.
- *(Vol) Volume:* The number of shares traded during a particular day. It is expressed in terms of hundreds or thousands of shares.
- *(YTD) Year to date percentage change (not shown):* The amount a particular share has gone up or down during the year expressed as a percentage of the closing price at the end of last year.
- *Other symbols:* There will usually be a legend to explain any other symbols used. The most common one '♣' indicates the annual report is available on request.

Interest rates

The interest rate a firm will have to pay in order to borrow money depends on two things: the risk-free interest rate in an economy and the credit worthiness (risk) of the particular firm.

Risk-free interest rates

- The committees that set monetary policy in each market (the 'Fed', Federal Exchange in the US; the 'MPC', Monetary Policy Committee in the UK; and the 'ECB', European Central Bank for the Euro currency) meet regularly to decide the rate at which they will lend money to the banking system. This determines short-term interest rates.
- Long-term interest rates are set by the market and are largely a function of the market's expectation of inflation and monetary policy in the future. Financial papers normally publish 10- and 30-year interest rates.

Credit risk

- Companies are graded in terms of how risky their debt is (i.e. how well they are able to pay back debt).
- The generic scale is: AAA, AA, A, BBB, BB, B, CCC, CC, C, D. An 'AAA' rating means the company is extremely safe and is very unlikely to default. A 'D' rating means that the company is bankrupt.
- Anything rated BB or below is called a "high yield" bond and anything rated BBB or above is called 'investment grade'.

Foreign exchange

The foreign currency markets are important factors in the import and export of goods and services and the flows of investments between countries.

- Exchange rates (the value of one currency in terms of another) between different currencies will often be displayed in a matrix form.

	USD	EUR	GBP
USD	1	0.909091	1.5
EUR	1.1	1	1.65
GBP	0.666667	0.606061	1

The convention of this matrix format is to express the currencies down the side in terms of the currencies across the top (in the example above 1 US Dollar = 1.1 Euros and 1 pound sterling = 1.5 US Dollars).

- Another way of publishing currency information is to express each currency in terms of one currency, normally US Dollars (GBP = 0.666667 in terms of 1 US Dollar).
- A third way is to use the following convention USD/EUR, where the first currency is expressed in terms of 1 unit of the second currency (e.g. USD/EUR = 0.909091).

Other important economic indicators

An economy is a complex collection of workers, raw materials, investment, consumers and companies. Creating a picture of a particular economy is difficult but the following indicators are commonly highlighted in financial newspapers as reflecting the health of a particular economy at a particular time.

GDP (Gross Domestic Product)

Gross domestic product measures the overall economic activity in an economy. GDP is important because it indicates the wealth of a nation (GDP per capita) and the economic health of the country. Activity in the economy can be measured in three ways: These three things are simply different perspectives on the same thing:

Output = Expenditure = Income.

– Output (the value of the total output of goods and services during a period)
– Expenditure (the total expenditure by governments, businesses and individuals on goods or services)
– Income (the total income to the government, businesses and individuals for providing goods and services).

Inflation

Inflation measures the cost of the same basket of goods and services at different points in time. An annual inflation rate of 10% means that the same basket of goods and services costs 10% more today than it did last year. In other words, it costs £1.1 to buy the same goods it cost £1 to buy last year.

This is a phenomenon that monetary policy-makers try to keep under control (inflation under 2% per annum is considered healthy for the economy).

Commodity prices

When the overall price of commodities (raw materials, e.g. copper, wheat) goes up significantly, this has a knock-on effect on the cost of production of other goods, which creates inflationary pressure.

Due to the importance of oil to consumers and manufacturers, this is the most commonly monitored commodity.

Unemployment

The unemployment rate is the percentage of people out of work versus the entire amount of people eligible for work. A high unemployment rate means an economy is not doing enough business to employ its potential workforce.

There is always likely to be some level of unemployment even in a strong economy.

8

Presentations

➡ Principles of good presentations

➡ Planning the presentation

➡ Writing the presentation

➡ Constructing slides

➡ Practising delivery

➡ Giving the presentation

Giving a presentation is an opportunity to show just how good your communication skills are. It is a chance to show your output to a large audience and is probably one of the fastest routes to success in most companies. This chapter outlines what makes a good presentation and shows you how to go about structuring and writing one. If the thought of giving a presentation makes you break out in a cold sweat, read the sections on dealing with nerves, delivering a presentation and handling questions. There are also sections on presenting as a team, impromptu speaking and attending presentations.

Principles of good presentations

It is not always obvious what separates good presentations from bad ones, but you will find that the good ones share a number of common characteristics. They all:

1. **Communicate the main point straight away.**
2. **Are short and to the point.**
3. **Are easy to understand.**
4. **Are easy to follow.**
5. **Have a good layout (and sound good if presented orally).**

If you still need convincing, take a look at the two examples below and see which is more efficient at getting the message across and which you would prefer to read.

Example 1

John,

I have just had a look at the schedule for Project X and there is no way that we are going to meet the deadline. We are already about three weeks behind and it is unlikely that, given the way things are, we can catch up.

As you know, Mary who works on accounts is due to go on maternity leave next week. This will put a further strain on the workload.

Remember when we met last week and you noticed how strained the atmosphere was; team morale is at an all time low. So many people are stressed out and upset that they have so much work to do and not enough time to do it.

For these reasons, I feel that we need another person on the team.

Mark

Example 2

John,

We need another person on the team. Here are the reasons:

1. We are 3 weeks behind the deadline for Project X.
2. Mary is due to go on maternity leave next week.
3. Team morale is low as everyone has too much work to do and too little time.

Mark

A good presentation does not happen by accident. It requires *planning, structuring, writing, editing* and, in the case of oral presentations, *rehearsing*. The remainder of this chapter deals with oral presentations but the approach and procedures for the most part apply equally to written presentations.

Planning the presentation

A little calm, clear thinking at the outset will save you a great deal of time later. Before you start writing, ask yourself the questions below. The answers to these questions will provide you with the information that will determine the language you use, how deep you need to go into the topic, what you say and how you say it.

Who is your audience?

- What is the general make-up of the audience (number, level, department)?
- What is their relationship with you and with each other?
- What is their current level of knowledge?
- How open are they to change or to new ideas?

Why are you giving the presentation?

- What is the objective of the presentation? (Do you want to argue, defend, educate, entertain, explain, induce action, inform, inspire, motivate, persuade? Or a mixture of these?)
- Were you given a brief?

What is the single most important message of the presentation?

- What is the *one thing* you want everyone in the audience to take home?

Where will the presentation take place?

- Will it be a formal or informal setting?
- Will it be a large or small venue?

When will it be given?

- How much time do you have to prepare it?
- At what time of day will the presentation take place?

How will it be presented?

- Will it be an oral presentation (with slides that will illustrate what you have to say), a written report (a stand-alone document) or a combination?
- It is a good idea to write a detailed document and then simplify it (by removing detail and magnifying the text and graphics) so that you have two documents: one that works as a paper that can be distributed after the presentation and the other as a set of visuals for your presentation.

Structuring the presentation

At school, you probably learned to structure essays as follows: brief introduction followed by arguments that logically lead to a conclusion. However, most people don't have time to wade through arguments to find out what they need to know; if they don't get the message in the first few minutes, they might never get it.

Minto's Pyramid Principle

Barbara Minto suggests an approach to structuring presentations that she calls 'The Pyramid Principle' from her book of the same name. There are two basic underlying ideas:

1. **Every presentation can and should be reduced to a single main message.**
   - The pyramid is used as a thinking tool. Start from the bottom of the pyramid and work upwards. The pyramid will have the main message at the top of the pyramid with all the ideas supporting it underneath.
2. **The main message should be stated as soon as possible, preferably immediately after a short introduction.**
   - The pyramid is used as a communication tool. Start from the top with the main message and work down to the key points and supporting detail.

   Use the structure below (Figure 8.1) to help you write the presentation.

- Start off with an Introduction that sets the context for the presentation and states the main message.
- Support what you have said in the main body of the presentation.
- Finish up with a summary and an outline of the next steps to be taken.

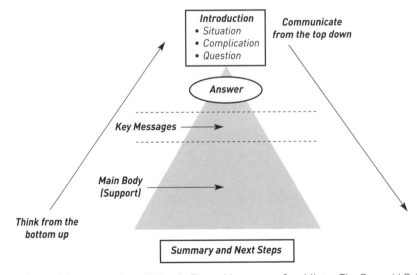

Figure 8.1 A visual interpretation of Minto's Pyramid concept. See Minto, *The Pyramid Principle* for more details.

Writing the presentation

Once you have an objective, a structure and some basic data, you can start to write the presentation. Getting started is often difficult so try the following:

Go somewhere quiet

- Block a period of time during which you can write without any disturbance.

Write whatever comes into your head

- Let your thoughts flow on to the paper, leaving gaps that can be filled in later if necessary.

Write as you would speak and don't worry about how it sounds

- This stage is about getting your thoughts down, not about style.

Keep reminding yourself what the main message of the presentation is

The introduction

The introduction is the most important part of the presentation so spend plenty of time thinking it through.

State the situation

- Answer the who, why, what, where and when type questions.
- Ensure the audience starts from the same standpoint as you, the writer.
- Present facts that are indisputable and acceptable to your audience so you immediately establish a rapport.

Outline the complication

- State what happened that changed the situation. This is the complication and it should logically raise a question about what needs to be done.

Pose the question

- It is crucial that the audience is aware of what the presentation is trying to tell them. If they aren't, they won't be able to absorb the answer to your question.
- Make sure you ask the right question, as the main part of the presentation will be spent addressing and hopefully answering the question.

Answer the question (main message of the presentation)

- Make sure your answer is short, relevant and action-oriented. The answer is the single most important message you communicate to the audience.
- The reader should be able to absorb the message in the first 30 seconds.

 TOP TIP
If you don't ask the right question, you won't get the right answer.

Introduction – Example

(*Situation*) Beta is one of our leading products. It has won numerous awards and has been the leading product in its category for the past five years. (*Complication*) The launch of Gamma last May (by our main competitor) has put pressure on Beta's market share. (*Question*) We were asked to determine how we could maintain our number one position in the marketplace. (*Answer/Resolution*) We have concluded it is possible by:

- Improving availability in rural areas.
- Launching Zeta, a complementary product to Beta.
- Increasing brand awareness among the under-25s sector.

TOP TIP
The key to a good presentation is setting things up properly in the introduction.

The body of the presentation

Once you have stated the main message of the presentation, you need to let your audience know either why what you said is true or how you are going to achieve what you said. The best way to do this is by logical argument:

Support the main message with some facts (or key messages)

- Try to have about five reasons (or key messages): any less and your support is too weak, any more and your audience will lose track.

Present all of the key messages on one slide

- Then take each of the messages and write a supporting slide (or two) for each one. (See p. 112 on constructing a slide.)

Don't be tempted to overload the slides with information

- It is your job to take all the information and make sense of it for your audience.

TOP TIP
The best presentations do not last longer than 20 minutes. Allowing at least one minute per slide, your presentation (including the introduction and conclusion) should have no more than twenty slides.

The summary and next steps

Never forget that no matter how interesting your presentation is or how well you present it, people will be pleased when it comes to an end. The ending, like the introduction, is when the audience's attention is at its highest, so you should spend some time crafting a good one. The end of a presentation has two main functions:

Summarize what has been said already

- Put the main message and major points on a slide. No new information should be included.

Gather momentum for what is to happen next

- Create a slide with a timeline and general outline of what you hope to do over the coming months. The end of a presentation usually signals the start of an initiative, so present this action programme at the end.

Editing the draft

The first draft is all about the ideas and structure of the document. When you have come up with a draft presentation, it is time to fashion it into an attractive, readable docu-

TOP TIP
It is not enough to inform the audience of something; they must be told what they need to do with the information.

ment. When you have finished this, take a break before you start editing. There will be lots of choices to make and making them will not always be easy; you will have to be ruthless. Consider the following:

Introduction

- Is your opening interesting/engaging?
- Is your purpose defined?

Body

TOP TIP
Stop editing when you start making changes that don't justify the time.

- Is the message clear, relevant and insightful?
- Is the structure logical?
- Is the content relevant and compelling?
- Does your tagline state your message and read like a story?
- Are transitions and set-ups smooth?
- Is your language clear and concise?
- Is your tone appropriate?

Ending

- Is the review concise?
- Are the next steps clear?

General

- Is there a balance between words and pictures?
- Are your font, background, graph type and structure consistent?
- Are you using the most appropriate word? Is it spelt correctly?

Constructing slides

As mentioned at the beginning of the chapter, it is best to write your presentation so that it can work as a stand-alone document (i.e. it has all the information a reader would need) and then go through it and simplify it for presenting. You should end up with two documents: one that works as a paper that can be distributed after the presentation and the other as a set of visuals for your presentation.

A slide should be made up of a message and support for that message. The message takes the form of a 'tagline' or sentence which should appear at the top of the slide. Beneath the tagline, there should be some support for the point being made (see p. 109).

Taglines

The tagline should:

- Be a complete sentence.
- Be informative (i.e. don't just write a title).
- Communicate only one major idea.
- Be relevant.
- Make sense without any graphical support.
- Form a logical part of the story that is being told.

Support

The support should:

- Prove the point made in the tagline.
- Be simple and easy to read (don't fill the slide with information).
- Have immediate impact and be easily understood.
- Be matched to the data it is trying to prove.
- Be consistent with other slides in the presentation in terms of font (type, size and colour), colour scheme, layout and scales.

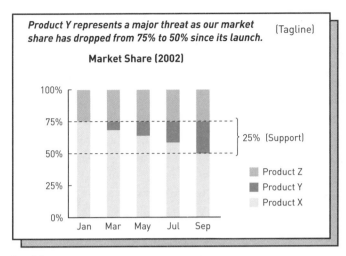

Figure 8.2 Sample slide

The biggest mistake that people make when creating slides is that they don't go through that second phase of simplifying the slides and end up presenting slides that are far too detailed. Remember that people are there to listen to you, not to read slides. Keep your slides simple:

Remove unnecessary detail

- Reduce the number of words on the slide.
- Remove all sources and footnotes.

Magnify the text

- The font should be 10 points for handouts and at least 18 points for a slide show presentation.

Magnify the graphics

- Make sure you can see every graphic from the back row of the audience.

Change the background and text colour

- Use a dark background with light text for a slide show presentation.
- Use a light background with dark text for handouts.

Keep colour to a minimum

- Use no more than 3–4 colours throughout the presentation.

TOP TIP
Keep slides clean and simple. Add the detail when you speak.

Types of support

A good visual can really enhance a presentation; a poor or irrelevant one can ruin a presentation, so keep your visuals simple and clear. You can make a presentation more interesting if you vary the type of support you use. Consider the following:

Bullet points

- Start all the points in the same way (e.g. all with a verb in the same tense).
- Ensure each point conveys a complete thought. Avoid slides that just list words (e.g. Plan, Implement, Assess).
- Never make more than five points.
- Keep slides with bullet points to a minimum; you are there to provide the words.

Tables

- Keep them simple and concise. Only use essential information.
- Confine them to one page.
- Order by columns rather than row, as columns are easier to read.
- Order columns by importance or by size.

Pictures

- Avoid using standard Microsoft clipart. Try to create something original.
- Ensure the pictures keep the tone of the presentation (e.g. don't use cartoons in a serious presentation).

Diagrams

- Make them appropriate; form should never become more important than content.

Videos

- Having video inserts in your presentation gives variety and helps keep your audience focused.
- Make sure all the technology you plan to use is working The more technology you use, the greater the chance of something going wrong and if something does go wrong, you could end up looking foolish and unprofessional.

TOP TIP
A few excellent slides will have more impact than lots of mediocre ones.

Graphs

- Don't insert a graph for the sake of it, as an inappropriate use of a graph adds nothing to a presentation.
- Use the graph that best shows the point you are trying to make. Remember that it is the *message* you want to get across and not the data that determines the type of graph you use.

CHECK LIST Which Type of Chart?

To show:
- ✓ The breakdown of a total: Use a pie chart.
- ✓ How things rank: Use a bar chart.
- ✓ The relationship between two variables: Use a paired bar chart.
- ✓ How something changes over time: Use a column or line chart.

Creating graphs

- Keep graphs simple; there should be just one message per graph.
- Give each graph a meaningful title.
- Use colour for emphasis, not to make them look pretty.
- State the units used (are you dealing with tens, thousands or millions?).
- Source the data.
- Don't clutter the slide with unnecessary notes.

Data points

- Ensure data groups are discrete (e.g. 1–10, 11–20 *not* 1–10, 10–20).
- Make the data points neat and easy to read (e.g. list them in increasing or decreasing order).
- Emphasize the most important segment or line.
- State the number of data points used underneath the graph (e.g. n = 10).
- Limit the number of data groups to six. (Take the five most important and group the remaining items as 'other'.)

TOP TIP

Use the strongest colour for the most important data and position it against the 12 o'clock segment in the case of pie charts and against the baseline in bar and line charts.

Practising delivery

When the presentation is written, there is still much to be done before it should be delivered to an audience. The more formal the situation, the more preparation should be done, but even an informal presentation should be rehearsed before delivery. Try to run through the presentation at least once.

Rehearsing

To give a successful presentation you need to be in control of your material, yourself and your audience. This is a lot to manage, so try to gain mastery of your material and yourself beforehand, and concentrate on the audience on the day.

Record yourself on video (or tape recorder)

- Look for your weak points and work on them but don't become too self-conscious.

CHECK LIST Dos & Don'ts of Delivering a Presentation

Do you:
- ✓ Mumble or talk too fast?
- ✓ Say 'er' and 'um' a lot?
- ✓ Fiddle with your pen or notes?
- ✓ Constantly use certain phrases?
- ✓ Turn your back on or ignore the audience?
- ✓ Pace up and down the floor?

Rehearse out loud

- Time your presentation from beginning to end. It will take longer than you expect.
- Leave a few minutes spare so you don't race through your presentation (e.g. if you have a 20 minute slot, make it a 17 minute presentation).

Rehearse as if it were the real thing

- Run right through without skipping sections and use your notes and aids.
- Rehearse at the venue, if possible.

Rehearse with a friend

- Ask someone who can give you constructive feedback to listen to you.

Rehearse as if everything were to go wrong

- Plan what you would do if you had no visuals, or your time was cut short.

TOP TIP
Always be ready to deliver the presentation on which you are working, as it is quite common for presenters to be unavailable at the last minute.

TOP TIP
Don't memorize your presentation word for word; it may end up sounding unnatural.

Speaker notes

If you are confident and feel comfortable with your material, it may be possible to present without using notes, but in general it is a good idea to prepare speaker notes and have them to hand. If you use notes, make sure you don't end up reading them to the audience. Your notes should be:

Short

- Use bullet points, key words, triggers or cues rather than sentences. This way, you will think about what you are saying and sound more convincing.

Easy to follow

- Use extra large type, upper- and lower-case writing, double spacing, highlighted words, one topic per card and number your cards.
- Keep them loose, never stapled.

Discreet

- You should be able to hold them in one hand only and at arm's length, so you maintain eye contact with the audience.
- Never use A4 sheets.

TOP TIP
If you are stuck for time, just make notes for the opening and closing of the presentation, as these are the most important times for making an impression.

Tips for rehearsers

If someone asks you to listen to their presentation:

- Be sensitive: Remember the presentation is tomorrow and this is not the time to undermine the presenter's confidence.
- Be constructive: Don't state a problem without a suggested solution.
- Be objective: Don't make remarks about things that will not make any difference to the message or the audience.
- Be realistic: Help the presenter concentrate on only those changes about which something can be done.

Dealing with nerves

It is normal, even important, to feel nervous before a presentation. If you don't feel worried at all, you may not be taking the presentation as seriously as you should and are more likely to make mistakes (unless you are a seasoned presenter). Having said that, nerves, if not controlled, can ruin your presentation, so let the adrenalin flow.

Reasons we feel nervous and how to cope

Most of us feel nervous because we are worried that:

We will come across badly

- Remember that no one is perfect; you are allowed to make mistakes. Try to be natural; don't try to be someone that you are not.

We will forget what to say

- Practise, practise, practise until you know your material inside out.
- Write out some speaker notes.

We won't be able to answer people's questions

- Admit it if you don't know the answer. No one expects you to know everything. Say that you will find out the answer and follow up with the person after the presentation.

We won't be able to deal with the unknown when it crops up

- Accept that the unknown probably *will* crop up, so just try to stay calm when it does.

Something will go wrong with the technology

- Make sure you know whom to contact and that you have their contact details.
- Have handouts of the presentation ready, so the show can still go on.

Someone will spot a mistake on the slide

- Don't be embarrassed, just thank them for pointing it out to you and correct what it should say.
- Try to keep mistakes to a minimum by asking someone to proofread your presentation.

TOP TIP
Remember that no one is perfect and there is no shame in making a mistake.

Tips for controlling nerves

Before the presentation

Visualize success

- Visit the venue if possible, or get a fax of the room layout. Picture yourself standing at the podium or on the stage, speaking to the audience.

Arrive early

- Make sure you can work the equipment.
- Make sure you have everything that you need.

Talk to the audience

- Try to meet and chat to the audience beforehand, as this will help break down any barriers between you and the audience.

Avoid drinks

- Avoid caffeine or very cold drinks just before speaking, but do try to have something light to eat.
- Go to the toilet before you go on stage.

Breathe

- Do some deep breathing exercises.
- Do some cardiovascular exercise that morning.

Take some time on your own

- Find somewhere quiet where you can spend some time on your own to think through the presentation.

During the presentation

Compose yourself

- Walk calmly to the stage, organize your notes, look out to the audience and smile. Then take a deep breath and start.

Slow down

- Don't rush the presentation. Think of it as a conversation with the audience.

Think positive

- Keep in the back of your mind how impressed everyone will be if you give a great presentation, not how unimpressed they will be if you don't.

Find a friendly face

- Find support in a friendly face until you are composed.

Preventing disasters!

Before the event, make sure you have:

1. **The correct version of the presentation.**
   - Keep version control of the document. Every time you save, save the version (e.g. document name V1 or V2).
   - Consider putting the version in a small font on the bottom right hand corner of each slide.

2. **Back-ups of the presentation.**
   - Save the presentation on the hard drive.
   - Put it on a floppy disk.
   - Email it to yourself.
   - Print it out. Photocopy any handouts that you need.

> **TOP TIP**
> Never leave copying until the last minute as invariably photocopiers get jammed, run out of paper or take ages to warm up.

3. **Time with the publishing department (if relevant).**
   - Book enough time if you are having your presentation professionally published (many companies have in-house departments). Try to book at least a week before you need it. Don't come at the last minute and expect to be facilitated.
   - Organize overtime help early if you think you will need it.

4. **Checked the room.**
   - Are there enough chairs?
   - Can everyone see the screen? Place it at an angle (not directly in front of) your audience. Check if you can read the slides from the back of the room.
   - Is there a podium? Can it be moved?
   - Are the lights working?
   - Is the temperature all right? Make sure it is neither too hot nor too cold.
   - Is there the appropriate technology (including connections)? Is it working? Run through procedures with the technicians.

5. **Booked all the things you need.**
   - Organize overhead projectors, flip charts (and markers) or a screen with connections for your laptop if you need them.
   - Organize beverages for the break, if appropriate.

6. **A list of what you need to take with you.**
   - Laptop and relevant connections if appropriate.
   - Material for the presentation (e.g. slides, acetates, videos, models).
   - Back-up material (e.g. floppy disk, handouts in case of technical failure).
   - Details of people you can contact if you have other requirements on the day (e.g. who can change the room temperature, get more chairs or sort out technical difficulties).

Giving the presentation

Never forget that the people in the audience probably dislike having to be there, even more than you dislike having to present. When people come to a presentation, they come *prepared* to listen. Your aim, as the presenter is to make them *want* to listen. You have succeeded if you have grabbed and held the audience's attention and they have understood everything you said.

Presentation sequence

A good presentation, like a good story, must have a definite beginning, middle and end. A good story must also be simple, to the point and easy to remember. The best way to achieve this is through repetition:

1. Tell them what you are going to tell them (Introduction).
2. Tell them (Key messages and supporting data).
3. Tell them what you've told them (Conclusion).

> **TOP TIP**
> Always start your presentation on time. If key people come in late, give a quick summary of where you are and move on, but don't wait.

The opening

A strong opening is crucial for a successful presentation. If you don't create an impact and arrest the audience's attention from the word go, you will not be given a second chance. You need to connect with your audience from the start. Try to:

Grab the audience's attention

- Start the presentation with a quotation, story, fact or question.
- Be as enthusiastic as you want your audience to be.

Establish yourself as a credible and authoritative figure

- Say who you are and why you are speaking on this topic.

Address the audience directly

- Thank everyone for coming.
- Make it clear what participation you expect.
- Work to decrease the psychological divide that tends to exist between speaker and audience (e.g. never turn your back to the audience, avoid using 'I' and always use 'we' rather than 'you').

Outline the presentation format

- State what you are going to talk about and why.
- State when you will take questions.
- State if you will be handing out copies of the presentation.

Let people know the timing

- State how long the presentation will be and if there will be breaks.

The body of the presentation

During the body of the presentation you must lead the audience through a clear and logical argument. Make sure you:

Tell a logical story

- Present the points in the same sequence as outlined in your opening.
- Point out what each slide was designed to show (never put up a slide and take it down without explaining it).
- Relate each section to the big picture.
- Make it obvious when you are moving from one section to the next.

Keep your language simple

- Keep your sentences short and avoid idioms, slang or sarcasm, especially if you have an international audience.

Correct yourself if you make a mistake and move on

- Don't panic if you make a mistake, it happens to everyone at some time.

Watch the audience's reaction

- Keep an eye on your audience's reaction and adjust your presentation accordingly (e.g. if they look bored, change your tone or ask a question; if they look confused, restate what you have said in more simple terms).
- Give the audience time to digest the information on each slide before commenting on it.

Keep an eye on time to make sure you are on track

- Cut out the less important things if you are running out of time.
- Don't be afraid to finish early if you are getting through it sooner than planned.

Bring your presentation alive

- Bring the presentation alive through your voice and body language; people have come to hear you, not to read slides.

Voice

Volume

- Speak loudly enough to allow people in the back row hear you.
- Increase and decrease the volume of your voice to emphasize key points.
- Don't tail off towards the end of a point.

Pitch

- Avoid sounding monotonous by varying the pitch of your voice.
- Use downward inflections. They sound more confident and persuasive than upward inflections.

Pace

- Take care to speak more slowly than you would in an everyday context. Nerves often make people ramble, so make a conscious effort to slow down and speak clearly and distinctly.

Pause

- Don't be afraid of silence – the pause is an incredibly powerful technique.
- A good pause should be longer than you think is necessary.

Body language

Hands

- Keep your hands loosely by your sides.
- Don't cross your arms, put them behind your back, in your pockets, through your hair or on your hips.
- Don't fidget. Leave pens down unless you need to write something.

Eyes

- Look people in the eye; do not stare through them.
- Don't focus on just one person; look at several people, spending no longer than a few seconds on each.
- Look for a friendly face if the audience seems hostile.

Face

- Keep your head up. Smile and look happy to be there.

Movement

- Stand tall with equal weight on each foot. Never shift from foot to foot.
- Make the space around you your own and use it to narrow the psychological distance between you and the audience.
- Make any movement confident and deliberate.
- Be natural and let your personality come through. Don't force yourself to be too still and don't pace up and down.

The ending of the presentation

Make it obvious that you have reached the end of your presentation.

- Round off the talk with a summary of what you have already said.
- Draw some concrete conclusions or recommendations and suggest next steps.
- End on a high note.
- Thank the audience for listening and then open the floor to questions (you could take questions during the presentation but it can be distracting).

Answering questions

Open up the question session to everyone without exception and show everyone equal respect. Remember, there is no such thing as a stupid question. Plant someone in the audience with a question or have some questions up your sleeve in case no one asks one. This gives people time to compose a question of their own. When you are asked a question:

TOP TIP
Don't think of it as you versus them; the audience is not the enemy.

1. **Listen to the question.**
   - Give your full attention to the questioner.
   - Note down some points if the question is long or complex.
   - Do not start to answer until you are sure that the speaker has finished.

2. **Make sure you have understood the question before answering.**
   - Thank the questioner for their 'interesting' or 'important' question.
   - Paraphrase to ensure you have understood correctly and that everyone is aware of what the question is.

3. **Pause to think about the answer.**
   - Let the questioner know you are considering your answer.

4. **Answer.**
   - Look at the whole group when answering, not just at the questioner.
   - Relate the question back to the main message of your presentation.
   - Give a concise answer at a level appropriate to your audience. If a longer explanation is required, offer to speak to the questioner after the session.
   - Make sure that the questioner is satisfied with your response.

TOP TIP
When you start running out of time, signal that the next question will be the last. After you answer it, thank everyone for coming.

Dealing with difficult questions

Questions can often catch us out and make us feel ill at ease. It is imperative that you don't let your emotions take over. If this happens and you feel yourself getting angry or upset, take a moment to control how you feel before answering. You can buy yourself time by calmly asking the questioner to elaborate or refine their question.

If you can't answer the question:

- If you don't know the answer to a question admit it, but offer to find out the answer afterwards and do keep your promise.

TOP TIP
Anticipate the most obvious questions (think about who will be present and what departments they are from – people tend to ask questions related to their own specific field) and prepare responses, including back-up material, if appropriate.

If a question is asked before you deal with the topic:

TOP TIP
If someone is giving a speech when asking a question, end it diplomatically.

- Tell the questioner that you will be dealing with their point later and ask if they would mind waiting until then. It is very impressive if you remember to turn to the relevant person with the answer when you reach the appropriate topic.

If the question is awkward or irrelevant:

- Remain cool, calm and collected and ask if you could discuss it during the break (as time won't allow an appropriate answer).

If the question is aggressive or hostile:

- Show understanding for what the questioner is saying and try to find common ground.
- Depersonalize the question by either asking for an example or by rewording it in non-emotional language.
- Answer in a calm and objective way. Never raise your voice and argue or debate.
- Give a succinct answer and move on.

Presenting as a team

There may be occasions when you have to present as a team. If the occasion arises, keep the following in mind:

Have clearly defined roles

- Look and act like a team.
- Make sure everyone knows their role.
- Explain the different roles and why people are presenting different sections. If someone isn't presenting, make sure there is a reason for them to be there.

Create a seamless presentation

- Give someone the responsibility of making sure that the slides are consistently formatted.
- Make a smooth handover to the next speaker. Summarize your points and introduce the speaker and topic of the next section, at the end of your section. Never use clichés like 'So over to you John' or 'So, without further ado – Mary – go for it!'

Refer, support and repeat the central message

- Keep the 'argument' coherent, with each section logically moving on from the previous one and strengthening the overall message.
- Repeat your message. It is better to have each of the speakers talk on different aspects of the same theme than on separate themes.
- Support each other's arguments by referring back to them (e.g. 'As Kate said … ' or 'Let me add to what Will has told you'). Avoid saying things like 'I shan't bore you by repeating what Claire was saying'.

Look interested in what is being said

- When you are waiting to present or have finished presenting, give your full attention to the person speaking, even though you may know their speech off by heart. Never stare into the audience or shuffle through your notes.

TOP TIP
One theme repeated three times will have far more impact than three separate themes.

Impromptu speaking

A great impromptu speaker always sounds prepared. This may sound like a contradiction in terms but it can be achieved if you:

Know what you would say before you are asked

- Jot down (or imagine) what points you would make, if you were asked to speak.

Take your time

- Don't say the first thing that comes into your head. Decide what point you want to make before you say anything; silence is less embarrassing than rambling.

Make eye contact

- Speak *to,* not *at* the people in the room.

Keep it brief and to the point

- Make about three points, listing all of them first and then giving a quick summary on each one.
- Think of it as a mini-presentation that should be structured and well delivered.

TOP TIP

Collect examples, short anecdotes and quotations in a notebook and memorize them as it is impressive and professional looking if you can start an impromptu speech with a relevant one.

Attending presentations

When you start out in your career, you will probably attend more presentations than you give. There are certain things you should and should not do when invited to one.

CHECK LIST Dos & Don'ts

✓ Decide if it's relevant to attend.
✓ Confirm your attendance.
✓ Give your full attention to the speaker.
✓ Be able to summarize the presentation (speakers, main points, the outcome).
✓ Sit near a door if you have to leave early.

✗ Don't start a conversation or mutter asides with the people beside you.
✗ Don't show boredom (e.g. sigh or yawn loudly).
✗ Don't ask awkward, irrelevant, aggressive or hostile questions.
✗ Don't air opinions later to selected colleagues that you were too cowardly to bring into open discussion.

Reading graphs

Don't just accept everything you see at face value, especially when you are shown graphs. Everyone likes to show things in their best light, but that often means that certain truths are hidden. Make sure you:

Check the scale for distortions. Has it been:

– Expanded to make something look bigger?
– Contracted to make something look smaller?
– Inverted to make a fall look like a rise?

Consider what may have been left out

– Two points on a line showing a rise might cover up a steep fall in between.
– What happened before the start of the graph?

Check values for appropriateness

– Have two data sets been converted to base 100? (i.e. making the first number equal 100 and changing the rest accordingly). If so, it can be very misleading as both sets of data converge on the base.

TOP TIP
Don't be fooled by graphs. Ask yourself:

● What exactly is being graphed?
● What are the units on the axes?
● What could the graph be hiding?

III

THE
PEOPLE

- ➡ Working in a team
- ➡ Managing your boss
- ➡ Managing your customers
- ➡ Managing yourself

CHAPTER 9

Working in a team

→ Performance

→ Managing a team

→ Project management

→ Effective decision making

→ Overcoming team problems

Not everyone finds working in teams easy. Some people absolutely hate working with others, preferring to carry out tasks from start to finish on their own. They hate the slow decision-making process and the fact that others don't meet their standards. The bad news for these people is that companies place a lot of importance on teamwork and regard how people behave within teams as crucial to their advancement. This chapter will help you become a better team player by helping you identify your role and outlining your responsibilities if you are a team leader. There is also advice on managing projects, making decisions and overcoming some of the most common problems found in teamwork.

Performance

Belonging to a team that performs well is essential for your personal success. If you work in a team that has a great reputation, you will share the reputation of your team. Conversely, if your team is perceived as ineffective and going nowhere, you too will be tarred with the same brush, irrespective of how good you may be. Many companies reward employees based on their team's performance, rather than on individual performance, so being in a high-performing team is crucial. Understanding what makes a team work well and how much you can influence the performance of your team is important.

Effective teams share the following seven traits:

1. **Shared goals.**
   - Everyone is working towards a common goal.
   - People do not have hidden agendas.

2. **Productivity.**
   - The team doesn't waste time and gets the work done. Deadlines are met.

3. **Division of roles.**
   - There are clear divisions of labour and everyone knows what their roles and responsibilities are.
   - People work outside their role when necessary to make sure things get done.

4. **Clear communication.**
   - There is an open channel of communication where all ideas are considered and problems discussed and resolved.
   - Everyone gets a chance to speak and when someone speaks, everyone listens.

5. **Personal growth and recognition.**
   - People are individually praised both within the team and publicly for the work they do.
   - People have mentors and are given opportunities for growth.

6. **Team spirit and respect for one another.**
   - There is a good relationship between all members. Everyone supports and is sympathetic to one another. Working with one another is enjoyable.

7. **Openness to people outside the team.**
   - The team never becomes a clique that refuses outside input, influence and criticism.

Being an effective team player

Even if you do not work in a formal team, you will work in a team to some extent. You are not an island; you will have to do things with others, so it makes sense to consider how you can excel in a team environment and help your team to maximize its potential. Your attitude is of paramount importance:

Attitude to work

Be enthusiastic about the job

- Take and show a genuine interest in what your team is doing.

Be clear what your role and responsibilities are

- Question the team leader until you know what is expected of you.

Take the initiative

- Don't wait to be told what to do.
- Work to improve how things are done.

Be reliable

- Deliver quality work and get the job done.
- Never make promises you can't keep.

TOP TIP
Communicate what you can give and what you want from the team with the team leader.

Attitude to other team members

Respect everyone

- Find common ground with each colleague.

Be open-minded

- Keep an open mind to all ideas and viewpoints.

Try to understand everyone's strengths and weaknesses

- Try to understand how members like to work.

Encourage and praise your team mates' work

- Help your team members to grow by providing encouragement and feedback.
- Be sincere. Don't go overboard with praise.

Attitude about self

Have a positive attitude

- Focus on solving problems rather than administering blame.

Be selfless

- Help those who are struggling with their responsibilities.

Be open to learning and feedback

- Own up to your mistakes. Accepting that you are not perfect is the sign of a strong character, being defensive is not.

Team roles

People often adopt different roles in a team. They tend to be the roles that suit their personality best. Dr Meredith Belbin has come up with a comprehensive list of team roles and this list is often used in business. A very effective team will contain one person in each of these roles but difficulties may arise if the team is made up of mainly one type. Figure out which one you are naturally drawn to:

1. **The Plant.**

   Traits: Creative, imaginative, unorthodox.

   Contribution: Solves difficult problems.

   Weakness: Ignores incidentals. Too preoccupied to communicate effectively.

2. **The Resource Investigator.**

   Traits: Extrovert, enthusiastic, communicative.

   Contribution: Explores opportunities. Develops contacts.

   Weakness: Over-optimistic. Loses interest once initial enthusiasm has passed.

3. **The Coordinator.**

   Traits: Mature, confident, a good chairperson.

   Contribution: Clarifies goals, promotes decision making, delegates well.

   Weakness: Can be seen as manipulative. Offloads personal work.

4. **The Shaper.**

   Traits: Challenging, dynamic, thrives on pressure.

   Contribution: The drive and courage to overcome obstacles.

   Weakness: Prone to provocation. Offends people's feelings.

5. **The Monitor-Evaluator.**

   Traits: Sober, strategic and discerning.

   Contribution: Sees all options. Judges accurately.

   Weakness: Lacks drive and ability to inspire others.

6. **The Team Worker.**

   Traits: Cooperative, mild, perceptive and diplomatic.

   Contribution: Listens, builds, averts friction.

   Weakness: Indecisive in crunch situations.

7. **The Implementer.**

   Traits: Disciplined, reliable, conservative and efficient.

   Contribution: Turns ideas into practical actions.

   Weakness: Somewhat inflexible. Slow to respond to new possibilities.

8. **The Completer-finisher.**

   Traits: Painstaking, conscientious, anxious.

   Contribution: Searches out errors and omissions. Delivers on time.

   Weakness: Inclined to worry unduly. Reluctant to delegate.

9. **The Specialist.**

   Traits: Single-minded, self-starting, dedicated.

   Contribution: Provides knowledge and skills in rare supply.

   Weakness: Contributes on only a narrow front. Dwells on technicalities.

TOP TIP

An excellent team player will identify the different roles that are present in their team and will adopt a role (one that doesn't necessarily come most naturally), just to give the team balance.

Managing a team

One of the most obvious roles in any team is that of team leader and just as there are natural team players, so there are also natural leaders. However, some of the best leaders are people who are not necessarily natural leaders but who have worked on their leadership skills. How people lead depends on themselves, the people they are in charge of, and how developed the team is; as the team gains skills and gets used to working with each other, the role of the leader must change.

Responsibilities of a team leader

1. **See the big picture.**
   - Understand what needs to be done.
   - Create an action plan and prioritize goals.
   - Manage the team's workload. Don't be afraid to stand up to those more senior than you, if your team is being asked to do too much. You need to make sure that you allow the team members to balance their work and life.

2. **Delegate the work.**
   - Discuss the needs of individuals and the team as a whole.
   - Establish roles and responsibilities based on members' current skills, desires, areas for growth and workload.

   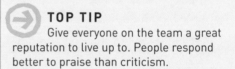

   TOP TIP
   Give everyone on the team a great reputation to live up to. People respond better to praise than criticism.

   - Spend time providing context and making it clear exactly what you want from each person. Make sure expectations are mutually understood.
   - Don't delegate work with specified methods to be followed; if possible, give people scope to come up with their own approach.

3. **Motivate the team.**
   - Foster a team spirit where people are working for the good of the team not themselves. Never reward someone for looking good at the expense of someone else.
   - Get everyone involved and agreed on the team goal, irrespective of level. Find out what motivates each team member.

4. **Coach team members.**
   - Develop the people on the team by providing feedback on their work, suggesting improvements and creating opportunities.
   - Always support your team, especially at times of failure or difficulty.
   - Don't pounce on mistakes; be subtle and make them seem easy to rectify.
   - Work on developing your team through encouragement, not criticism.

5. **Resolve issues.**
   - Make sure the team is always content by resolving any internal or external issues as they arise.

CHECK LIST
- ✓ Deal with issues sensitively.
- ✓ Be collaborative, not confrontational.
- ✓ Start by asking questions, not making statements. This will push the onus back on the team and soften the blow of criticism.
- ✓ Be descriptive when commenting on what happened, not judgemental.
- ✓ Be specific about what the problems are and give concrete examples.
- ✓ Let people save face.

6. **Ensure deadlines are met.**
   - Make sure everyone knows when work must be completed.
   - Encourage honesty and open communication where everyone feels comfortable raising issues, especially pertaining to work status.

MIND YOUR MANNERS!
Don't forget to say thank you.

7. **Ensure quality.**
   - Make sure the quality of the work is of a high standard by constantly monitoring the work being done.

8. **Communicate work status.**
   - Communicate the team's results and findings to senior people.
   - Praise your team to senior people. Complaining about the team will reflect badly on you.
   - Keep the team informed on an informal basis. A brief, weekly status meeting is a good idea.

9. **Give and encourage feedback.**
   - Conduct reviews promptly.
   - Provide members with positive and constructive developmental feedback.
   - Create a continuous feedback loop and solicit upward feedback from team members to ensure you are performing your responsibilities well.
   - Act on any feedback you receive.

Project management

No matter what your current role is, there will be a time when you will have a project, however small it may be, to run. The responsibility for completing a task by a certain deadline, within a certain budget and possibly employing certain resources, may be a bit daunting. This section takes you step-by-step, showing you the way to achieve this.

The steps

1. **Establish who will take ultimate responsibility for the project.**

    *   Set up a meeting with the person responsible for the project (it is usually the person who provides the budget). Make sure you give yourselves plenty of time; it is vital that this meeting is not rushed.

    *   Don't leave this meeting without getting a clear and measurable objective for the project; starting a project with no clear vision of its end-goal is a recipe for disaster.

    *   Work out who else will need to be involved in the project and who has a vested interest in the outcome (i.e. the stakeholders).

    *   Meet each person individually and, if possible as a group, so that everyone is clear about what the project is trying to achieve. It may be difficult to get agreement but it is easier to handle conflicts before you start a project than during it.

TOP TIP
Stand up to your sponsor until you know exactly what they want. This firm push back may annoy the sponsor now but it will be appreciated later.

2. **Write down what you need to do.**

    *   It is absolutely essential that you know exactly what you are trying to achieve from the outset; you need to know where you want to get to, in order to figure out the best way to get there. By writing the objective of the project down, you will force yourself to see if you completely understand what you are being asked to do and what the point of the project is. If you are not sure, now is the time to get it cleared up.

CHECK LIST
Before each stakeholder meeting is over, make sure you:
*   ✓ Get each person on your side.
*   ✓ Find out exactly what they want the project to achieve.
*   ✓ Find out how they will measure the project's success.
*   ✓ Get a provisional budget allowance.
*   ✓ Get them to agree to help where they can.
*   ✓ Arouse their enthusiasm for the project.

3. **Double-check your understanding of the project's objective.**

   - Create a scope document underlying your understanding of what is in and out of scope for the project and email it to your sponsor. Ask him/her to let you know if this is also his/her understanding of the project outcome. It is good to put this in writing.

4. **Write a plan.**

   - Don't panic. Planning is critical; a little thought up front will save you a lot of time later on.
   - Write down whatever needs to be done to arrive at the final objective. Force yourself to think about measurable business results (the 'what' needs to be achieved), rather than activities (the 'how' it will be achieved). Don't worry about accuracy or neatness, you can reorganize it later.
   - Refine this list (e.g. group work that could be done together, sequence tasks and check if there are ways of getting several things done in parallel).
   - Prioritize the work and create milestones (smaller goals) you need to achieve.

5. **Build contingency into the plan.**

   - Understand what cannot be compromised on your project in terms of time, cost or quality. Problems generally affect projects in one of these three ways: the project will take longer, it will cost more or the quality of the work will suffer.

    CHECK LIST

   Your plan should state:
   ✓ How long the project will take (time needed).
   ✓ How much work is involved (resource required).
   ✓ How much it will cost (budget needed).

   - Work out the risks involved in the project, how likely they are to occur, how you would deal with them if they did, and how much they would cost you. It is essential to build contingency into your plan because no matter how hard you work, there will always be surprises. The standard contingency figure is about 15% of the total budget figure.

    **MORE INFO?**
   See p. 83 for more on budgeting.

   - Decide whether you want to show contingency explicitly or hide it.

6. **Get your plan signed off.**

   - Send the plan to your sponsor for approval. Make sure it clearly outlines the objectives of the project, the budget, resources and time required.
   - Be ready to negotiate (e.g. if they want you to do it sooner, negotiate more resources, if they want to cut budget, revise down the scope).
   - Make sure you get written approval for the version of the plan from which you will work – it will resolve any misunderstandings about scope later.

7. **Delegate the work.**
   - Understand the team's capabilities and assign the work appropriately.
   - Make sure everyone understands and agrees to their responsibilities.
   - Manage each person according to their needs.

8. **Make sure the work gets done.**
   - Check up on everyone's progress. Never assume that just because people know what they have to do, that it is being done.

CHECK LIST

Hold a weekly status meeting:
- ✓ Keep the meetings short and sharp.
- ✓ Don't let people ramble on about what they have been up to, just ask them to compare where they are today to where they should be today.
- ✓ Encourage them to be honest about where they are in their work and to alert you to delays as soon as they occur. Get them to be realistic about how much longer their section will take.
- ✓ Email the agreed next steps to the team (with names and dates for every action) after the meeting.

9. **Keep re-prioritizing.**
   - Keep asking yourself what you are trying to do and whether that is still what everyone wants. You need to keep alert to make sure you know when things change because invariably things do change.
   - Maintain a healthy insecurity about the project. Even if things are going well, you shouldn't rest on your laurels as situations can change quickly.
   - Create an Issue and Risk log and update it at the weekly status meeting.

10. **Tell people what is happening.**
    - Don't avoid bad news. Manage expectations throughout the project, not just two weeks before the deadline.
    - Make sure you could say what the project is about and what the current status is if you are asked. This should take no longer than 5 minutes.

CHECK LIST

Avoid detail. Only tell people what they need to know:
- ✓ *Project results:* Will the project objective be met? If not, what can your sponsor expect? Will what is achieved meet his/her needs?
- ✓ *Time:* Is it on time? If not, how much longer will it take?
- ✓ *Budget:* Is the project over, under or on budget?

- Keep your sponsor and stakeholders informed of the project's progress by creating a weekly status report. Using traffic lights (Green = completed; Amber = underway/issues; Red = not started) is a simple and affective way to communicate status on each piece of work.

Success strategies

Keep things simple

- Look for a simple solution. Always ask yourself 'Is there a simpler way?'
- Focus only on the things that make a difference to the end result.
- Force yourself to look at the bigger picture. Too much information can confuse, so check regularly that you haven't got caught up in the detail.

Get and keep people on your side

- Most problems that arise stem from people, so think about everyone who will be affected by the project, what their likely position would be, and go around every one individually to get their support. Try to see things from their point of view.
- Be reasonable with your expectations and show your appreciation.
- Be appropriate in your leadership style and even if you start to feel stressed, never take it out on people working for you; they are probably working hard enough and more stress will have a negative affect.
- Try to create a good atmosphere; muck in when necessary and boost morale by buying pizza for lunch or ice pops for everyone.

> **TOP TIP**
> Keep everyone motivated about the project; if people are positive about the project, they will help make it succeed.

Learn to delegate

- Delegate as quickly as possible so that people have the maximum amount of time to get the work done.
- Spend your time managing your team, not doing things they could.

Don't get stuck in a rut

- Don't waste time pursuing a strategy that isn't working; think of other ways to get to the same end goal.

Visualize what the end result of the project looks like

- Imagine what success of your project looks like.
- Imagine all the possible obstacles and how you can overcome them.

Learn about the experience

- Learn from others' experience. Try to understand what made their project successful/unsuccessful.
- Learn about the project as you go along. Don't wait until the end to do a postmortem, instead insist on learning lessons as you go along (perhaps done in conjunction with the weekly status meeting) to give your team the opportunity for ongoing improvement.

Effective decision making

One of the toughest things a team leader has to do is make decisions. The process outlined below should make it somewhat easier:

1. **Think through all the elements of the decision.**
    - What is the decision?
    - Why do you need to make the decision?
    - Who needs to be involved in making the decision?
    - Does the decision depend on another decision that hasn't yet been made?
    - By when does this decision need to be made?

2. **Gather the facts.**
    - Work out what information you need to make an informed decision and what information you have.
    - Decide where the most reliable and easy place to find each piece of information is.
    - Restrict your fact-finding time to about an hour and a half.

3. **Consult other people.**
    - Choose the people you consult carefully. It is not very efficient speaking to everyone, so try to get a good spread of opinions so that most people are represented.
    - Speak to people who will be affected by the decision. You will need their support if the decision is to work.
    - Speak to your boss, even if only briefly. Most bosses like to know what is going on and to feel that they are involved.
    - Speak to senior people who have the power to help make things work out and those who will be upset if they are not consulted.

> **TOP TIP**
> Don't let lack of information prevent a decision. A decision made on partial knowledge is better than not making a decision at all, when one is required.

> **TOP TIP**
> Keep a record (e.g. email with your understanding of their opinion) of what people say, just in case they change their mind, post-decision.

4. **Identify the options.**

   - Come up with as many options as possible. You should always aim to have at least three options so that you don't have an either/or situation. The more choices you develop, the better the decision you can make.

5. **Choose an option.**

   - List the available options. Weigh up the pros and cons of each option and try to anticipate the likely outcomes for each.

   TOP TIP
   Be careful not to jump to a conclusion, based on intuition. Use the information you have found to create as many options as possible and then review them methodically.

   - Choose the option that is most practical and least risky. Often the best option in theory may not be the best in practice, and sometimes your decision may be that you will do nothing at all.

   - Make a decision no matter how difficult it may be. You must accept that there will always be an element of risk in every decision you have to make.

6. **Sell the decision.**

   - Inform people who will be affected by the decision and get their agreement. Make sure you tell them personally as hearing things second-hand makes people feel insignificant and demotivated.

   TOP TIP
   If you are really unsure whether or not you are making the right decision, sleep on it for a night before communicating it.

7. **Implement the decision and abide by the consequences.**

   - Make sure the decision is put into action and the outcome monitored.

MORE INFO?
See p. 58 for more on problem solving.

Team decision making

Making decisions in a team further complicates the decision-making process. Often decision making becomes a political game and discussion descends into an argument. The only way to make it work is to:

Get everyone involved

- Try to prevent the decision process being used as a political struggle for power between different members or organizational constituencies. Don't make people feel like winners and losers.
- Be objective and listen to other people's rationale. Look for the best answer, irrespective of who comes up with it. Encourage other members based on merit not friendship.
- Don't dominate the discussion and make sure everyone has their say.
- If you are the leader, suspend your judgement and act as a process enabler.

Avoid arguing against decisions without a good reason

- Arguing just to win your point is not constructive. Conversely, you shouldn't give in to avoid conflict if you have a good point.

Decide what to do when the team reaches an impasse

- Move on to something else and revisit the point later.
- Allow the decision to be made either by the team leader or a simple majority (51%+ vote wins).

Overcoming team problems

Even if your team gets on really well together, problems will arise. If you are directly involved in a problem, your first step to resolving it is to acknowledge that the problem exists. Then you need to decide what you are going to do about it. You should never be embarrassed about raising an issue with someone, just be careful how you do it:

Who should you approach?

- Try to sort things out with the person first and allow some time for the situation to improve.
- Speak to the group leader or manager if things don't improve.
- Consider getting a skilled and objective outsider to spend a day with the team if the issue is affecting the whole team and the leader is unable to solve it. Elicit constructive feedback on where the issues lie and what needs to be done.

Why should you raise the issue?

- Think through what you are trying to achieve by raising the issue. Be able to communicate this reason to the person with whom you have an issue.

When should you raise the issue?

- Try to discuss it close to the event, but not during it, when emotions are high.

Where should you raise the issue?

- Find an appropriate place, where you can chat openly without worrying about being overheard.
- Never criticize anyone in public.

How should you raise the issue?

- Spend some time thinking through the facts first. Jot them down on paper if necessary.
- Anticipate the likely response and deliver your message appropriately.
- Be sensitive and balance both positive and negative feedback. Don't be overly critical.
- Be specific about what you think the issue is and what the person would need to do differently.

> **TOP TIP**
> Don't get personal. Concentrate on the issue that needs to be solved or an outcome that you want to achieve.

Typical problems and what to do

Lack of direction

If you are the team leader:

- Call a meeting to explain the roles and responsibilities of each team member. Make sure that all the team members know what they have to do.
- Monitor the work being done on a weekly basis.

If you are a team member:

- Raise the issue with the leader and ask for a team meeting to inform everyone on what the overall goals and deadlines of the team are.
- Ask for a clear definition of roles and responsibilities and make sure everyone knows what they have to do, by when and to whom they have to report.

Lack of productivity

If you are the team leader:

- Ensure that every piece of work has someone responsible for it and everyone knows who that person is.
- Explain the overall goal and deadlines of the team and get agreement by explaining how their work fits into the overall goal.
- Make sure people are happy with their work and discuss changes that may be necessary (too much work/not enough time, etc.).
- Review progress on a regular basis. Don't criticize but find out why the work hasn't been done.
- Encourage honesty so that issues can be identified and dealt with early. Do not criticize people for not reaching their targets, but get them to explain why they have not been reached and work together to find a way to avoid such problems in the future.
- Recognize people's achievements and thank them for their work.

If you are a team member:

- Make an effort to meet all of your deadlines.
- If you are feeling demotivated, discuss the reasons with the team leader and work together to find a way of improving your job satisfaction.

Personality clashes

If you are the team leader:

- Speak to both parties separately to understand why they are not getting on. Then speak to them together and ask what steps they are going to take to resolve the problem.
- Keep an eye on the situation to see how things improve and follow up with meeting both parties after a few weeks.
- Try to ensure that they work in completely different areas and have minimum interaction (if possible).

If you are a team member:

- Respect others even if they are very different to you. Try to find something you like or value about the person or some common ground between you.
- Try to resolve the issue sooner, rather than later. Confront the person and ask if he/she has issues with you. Be honest about the impact their behaviour has on you.
- Let the person know you want to understand their point of view. Don't just try to force them to understand yours.
- Speak to your team leader and let them know the situation. Don't badmouth the other person, just say you can't get on and ask if they could make sure you work in different areas.

Internal bullying

If you are the team leader:

- Make it clear that bullying is not acceptable and that people may confide in you and you will take appropriate action.

If you are a team member:

- Acknowledge the problem.
- Keep a record of the times you were bullied to support your case. If your health is suffering, get a letter from your doctor or psychiatrist.
- Try to become more assertive. Approach the bully calmly and rationally explain that you find his/her behaviour unacceptable. Give concrete examples of bullying incidents and how it made you feel.
- Speak with your team leader or mentor if speaking about it directly with the person that is bullying you is not possible.

> **MIND YOUR MANNERS!**
>
> Never let your clashes affect other team members or their work. Don't force people to take sides.

Groupthink *(group too friendly, not critical enough of their work)*

If you are the team leader:

- Create a desire for ongoing group improvement. The group should not believe that they are as good as it gets.
- Instil an atmosphere where constructive feedback is accepted and rewarded.

If you are a team member:

- Don't just accept ideas, encourage debate about issues and challenge people's points of view.
- Elicit opinions about your ideas.

Exclusivity *(group becomes too isolated)*

If you are the team leader:

- Create a team that includes people from outside the current team.
- Assign each team member an external group with whom they are responsible for maintaining relations.

If you are a team member:

- Actively go out and meet people outside the team (but inside the company); let them know what you are doing and get their input.
- Let your team members know you are meeting up with people outside the team and encourage them to do the same.

Working in a virtual team *(a team that exists across geographical boundaries)*

If you are the team leader:

- Make sure that everyone in the team has a common understanding of what the team's goal is, as it is this shared purpose that is the sole reason for the team's existence.

If you are a team member:

- Communicate frequently (using new computer and telecommunications technology) to make up for the limited face-to-face contact.

Working in cross-cultural teams

It is very likely that at some point in time you will work in a multicultural team. This may be a very different experience to working in a mono-racial team as people have different ways of approaching things, based on their cultural norms. Such teams can be incredibly effective, especially when the whole team adopts the best of all cultures. It is not always easy, but never forget to respect everyone and try to learn more about each other's culture.

CHECK LIST

Keep in mind the following potential differences between your own worldview and that of others:

✓ **Values**
- How important is the individual?
- How important is religion?
- How important are age and gender?
- How important are background, status and position?
- How important is appearance?
- How important are punctuality and time?
- How important is it to follow rules and regulations?
- How important are hierarchy and empowerment?

✓ **Attitude to work**
- What is the pace of life (work hours and breaks) like?
- What is the importance of work in overall lifestyle?
- Are foreigners feared, disliked or looked down upon?

✓ **Decision making**
- Is it consensus driven or directive?
- Is it rational or intuitive?
- Is it based on analytical or associative reasoning?
- Are negotiations adversarial? (Is compromise viewed as a sign of weakness?)

✓ **Communication**
- How direct is it? (Is saving face important? Is bluntness frowned upon?)
- What rules apply to the body (e.g. eye contact, touching, stance or personal space)?
- How formal is it? (e.g. titles, deferential or respectful tone and lexicon)

Approach to work

The 'Chaotic' Boss

This type of boss is very forgetful, has little appreciation of time and has so many jobs going at the same time, none of them gets the attention they need. You should:

- Be organized. Know where everything is and what is going on as you will probably end up having to sort things out.
- Follow up requests and suggestions you've made if you think they've been forgotten.
- Prompt frequently at meetings and anticipate what he/she needs.

The 'Organized' Boss

This type of boss usually focuses on one task at a time. He/she likes logic and order and is very aware of what needs to be done and by when. You should:

- Mirror their way of working by being organized.
- Be punctual and keep to schedules.
- Be systematic in your work.

Approach to management

The 'Control Freak' Boss

This type of boss always needs to know what you are doing and wants to be involved in every part of your work to ensure that everything is being done their way and to their standard. You should:

- Gain their approval by carrying out your work as laid down.
- Proactively provide regular updates.
- Slowly introduce other ways of doing things as you gain his/her respect.

The 'Hands Off' Boss

This type of boss doesn't interfere with your work; they just let you get on with the job. You should:

- Keep him/her informed but not annoyed with trivial matters.
- Show you can be trusted.
- Ask for help when you need it.
- Get him/her to sign your work off (preferably by email).

Raising issues

Sometimes, despite all your best efforts (and all of the advice given here), you just can't get on with your boss. Never forget that although it helps, you are not necessarily meant to like each other. You just need to be able to respect each other and get the job done. If things are really bad, you should meet with your boss to discuss the issues.

Tips for raising issues with your boss

1. Decide whether it's worth raising the issue.
   - Choose your battles wisely. Some things may be worth putting up with, if you are getting on well with your project.

2. Raise issues with your boss first.
   - Give your boss a chance to sort any problems out.

3. Choose an appropriate time and place to have a chat.
   - Conduct meetings in private.
   - Think how they would like to receive the feedback.

 CHECK LIST Dos & Don'ts for Raising Issues

✓ Give a balanced view. Say what works, as well as what doesn't.	✗ Don't complain unless you can suggest a solution.
✓ Be honest about how you would like to be treated.	✗ Never be aggressive. You are there to find a solution not assign blame.
✓ Listen with an open mind to what is said and try to see their point of view.	✗ Don't gather the views of other people and use them to attack your boss.
✓ Be solution- not problem-oriented.	
✓ Watch out for body language, which indicates how your boss feels.	✗ Don't gloat or patronize if your boss admits to doing something unacceptable.
✓ Summarize the actions you have decided on, to make sure that you are in agreement.	

4. Review and monitor the situation.
   - Acknowledge any effort that is being made and remember that people often revert to type when under stress.

5. Escalate the issue if the problem persists.
   - Speak to Human Resources about moving teams, departments and in the worst-case scenario, even leaving the job.

Typical issues and what to do

You are very lucky if your boss appreciates your full potential and rewards you appropriately. In general, you will need to be very vocal about what you want.

Work overload

Clarify expectations

- Make sure both of you have a clear understanding of exactly what you are expected to do. If you push for clarity, you often find that the issues have not been thought through. Don't waste time working until your boss knows what he/she wants.

Prioritize the work

- Help your boss prioritize your work into the 'Must do', 'Should do' and 'Nice to do'. Drop the 'Nice to do' unless you have a lot of time.

Raise the issue with your manager

- Present a record of the hours you have worked. Say that you are happy to take on occasional heavy workloads but that it should not be the norm.

Learn to say 'no'

- Be assertive when saying 'no'. Politely explain why you are unable to help out.
- Suggest an alternative way of getting the task done.
- Get a reputation for being fair, for helping out when you are able and saying 'no' upfront when you genuinely don't have the time. Constantly saying 'yes' will not necessarily enhance your reputation, in fact it will probably stress you and make it difficult for you to get your work done.

 CHECK LIST

When your boss asks you to do something, ask yourself:
- ✓ Is this part of my job?
- ✓ What would I gain (learn) by doing it?
- ✓ By when does it need to be done? (Be very careful about agreeing to do things far ahead of time.)
- ✓ If I say I will do it, how will it affect my current workload? Will I need to stay late/work weekends?
- ✓ Is it possible for someone else to do it?
- ✓ What will happen if I say 'no'? Will it affect my career?

Promotion or pay rise

Put a sound case together

- Explain why you believe you deserve a rise. Substantiate this with evidence of pay in similar jobs that are higher than yours. Outline specific work you have done or achieved that would merit a rise/promotion.
- Be realistic about your performance.
- Never demand a pay rise or promotion.

 CHECK LIST

Learn to deal with obstacles. If your boss:
- ✓ **Depends on you and a promotion would mean losing you.**
  - – Reassure him/her that you will help train up any replacement.
- ✓ **Hasn't the authority to make the decision.**
  - – Enlist his/her help to do everything possible to get the pay rise/promotion for you.
- ✓ **Doesn't believe you should get the pay rise/promotion.**
  - – Understand why and what you need to do in order to get it.
- ✓ **Never gives you credit and passes your ideas off as their own.**
  - – Make sure that you keep records that prove that they are your ideas.
  - – Discuss the problem with your mentor, or Human Resource representative in terms of how it will affect your promotion possibilities.

Holiday

Book the dates with your boss

- Book the dates well in advance.
- Confirm your dates on a written medium such as email to avoid any misunderstanding.
- Remind your boss when the holiday is coming up.

Ensure that everyone feels comfortable about you leaving

- Make sure there is someone who can handle any issues when you are not there. Plan for the worst-case scenario.
- Give yourself plenty of time to tidy up matters before you leave, so no one feels that things are out of control.

Training

Let your boss know how much can be gained from your development

- Emphasize how much better you could do the job with coaching.

Be persistent about being developed

- Training and development are essential in any job; it should not be considered a luxury.

Responsibility

If you want more:

- Don't complain about not having challenging work to do. Suggest specific pieces of work that you could do but be realistic about your capabilities.
- Suggest work-shadowing your boss/experienced colleague if they do a job that you would like to do. If you do this, make sure you still complete your normal tasks.

If you have too much:

- List all of your responsibilities and how much time you spend on each one. Go through the list with your boss saying what responsibilities you wish to keep and suggesting to whom you could delegate the rest.

Sexual harassment

Clearly and firmly let the person know that you find their behaviour offensive

- Sexual harassment can be blatant and direct or suggestive and indirect.

 CHECK LIST

Sexual harassment includes:
- ✓ Touching or brushing against a colleague inappropriately.
- ✓ Making remarks referring to a person's appearance in a sexual context.
- ✓ Commenting on a person's sex life or their sexual performance.
- ✓ Suggesting benefits for sexual favours.
- ✓ Making obvious sexual advances.
- ✓ Forcing yourself sexually on someone.

Know the procedures

- If the sexual harassment continues, find out what the company's policy is. If your company has one, it is essential to follow their procedures.
- Keep note of how you followed the procedures and what the outcome was.
- Don't be put off making a complaint if there is no company procedure.

 CHECK LIST

Document:
- ✓ Who did it.
- ✓ What they did.
- ✓ What provoked it.
- ✓ When it happened.
- ✓ Where it happened.
- ✓ If there were any witnesses.
- ✓ How it made you feel.

Collect evidence

- Keep note of the harassment. Documentation should take place at home.
- Find witnesses and other victims to prevent it being one person's word against another.

File a complaint

Bullying

Speak to the person who is bullying you

- Calmly explain that you find their behaviour unacceptable. Make sure your body language sends out signals of authority, not submission.
- Be able to give specific examples of their behaviour and why it is unacceptable. Make sure you have more than one example.

Make an official complaint if it continues

- Keep a record of when the bullying takes place and how it makes you feel.
- Speak to your mentor, a Human Resources representative or a trusted senior manager.

Raising issues about your boss

There are times when, despite great effort, you cannot establish a good working relationship with your boss and there is daily friction between you. If this happens, you will need to think about approaching a higher authority such as a senior manager, your mentor or someone in Human Resources. If you do, try to:

Depersonalize the issue

- Focus on how things need to change, not how terrible your boss is.

Have a detailed diary of the issues

- List what the issues are, when they occurred, the effect they have on you and what you have done to try to resolve them.

Be psychologically prepared

- Be ready to calmly defend your position. Your boss will not be pleased when he/she is called to account for his/her actions and will most likely ask to meet you. Do not be bullied into submission. You have gone this far; make sure the issues are sorted out.

Listen politely to your boss's side of the story

- Never forget that you are trying to solve a problem, not assign blame.

Remember your basic rights

- You should be fairly rewarded (in terms of pay, promotion, training and growth opportunities) for the work you do, irrespective of your sex, colour, religion or age.
- You should be allowed to enjoy a life outside work.
- You should not have to work under threat, abuse or any condition that affects your mental or physical well-being.
- You should not have to do anything with which you are morally uncomfortable.

Annual appraisal

Most companies have an annual appraisal where you sit down formally with your boss or mentor to appraise your performance for the previous year, discuss training needs and promotion possibilities. If you have a good ongoing dialogue with your boss, nothing that is said at this meeting should be a surprise to you. However, if it is your first appraisal, you may feel vulnerable. You should see the meeting as a two-way process; you are going to be assessed but you are also getting an opportunity to raise issues that you may have.

Prepare yourself prior to the meeting

 CHECK LIST

Create a list of:

✓ **Last year's work**
- Your greatest achievements during the past year.
- Areas (outside of current role) where you contributed to the organization.
- Significant issues you would like to raise (work-related problems you have).
- Feedback on your boss (it is not always asked for, but be ready just in case).

✓ **Next year's work**
- What your objectives for the coming year are.
- What skills you would like to develop/roles you would like to fill.
- What promotion opportunities and salary increases are open to you.

Get a copy of the company's promotion criteria (if this exists in written format)

- Measure yourself against each of the criteria.
- Be honest about how you did and what you think you need to do to ensure promotion.

Book a room for the meeting (if you are asked)

- Find somewhere that will allow a confidential, undisturbed conversation.
- Book for double the amount of time you think you will need so that you do not end up rushing the meeting.

Arrive on time and look prepared

Taking feedback

Use it to help you

- Look for practical suggestions and specific examples of what you could do to improve.
- Be objective and listen to what is being said. Use this criticism to help you become a great businessperson.

Take it on the chin

- It is a great trait to be able to accept another's appraisal and criticism of where and how you need to improve.
- Don't be deflated by it, remember that criticism is not an attack on your whole person.

Stand up for yourself

- Distinguish between constructive and destructive criticism. Accept and work on the former, ignore the latter.
- Do not be on the defensive but defend yourself when you think it is right. Don't accept criticism if you think it is unfair.

> **TOP TIP**
> A little modesty is fine, but don't be embarrassed when you are complimented on your work. Be gracious when you are praised.

Giving feedback

Think about what you are going to say

- If you are asked for feedback, say that you need time to think about the issues if your contribution is to be worthwhile. Settle on a date and time.

Focus on the problem, not the person

- Never attack someone personally.

> **TOP TIP**
> When someone says, 'Tell me what you honestly think', don't take it as an invitation to be frank.

Deal with what is achievable

- Don't raise an issue for which you can't think of a solution.

Be specific

- Avoid making vague comments; they aren't helpful.

> **TOP TIP**
> List three things the person does well and should continue to do and three things that need to be worked on.

11

Managing your customers

➡ Customer service habits

➡ Customer complaints

➡ Client knowledge

➡ Client entertainment

➡ Being a customer

Everybody has a customer, even those who have no contact with external clients. If somebody relies on you for services, products and information to get their job done, even though they may be colleagues, they are also your customers and like all customers, they expect good treatment. They constantly rate (albeit subconsciously) everything, so never underestimate the impact you can make. This chapter outlines the top ten things to do when dealing with customers and gives advice on dealing with complaints, learning more about your customers and attending hospitality events. Finally it gives some pointers on how you should behave if you are a customer.

Customer service habits

Numerous books have been written about how you should treat your clients, but here's a summary of the ten most important things to consider:

1. **Treat the customer as the most important part of your job.**
   - Make your customers feel valued and important and do everything you can to serve them the way they want.
   - Never treat a customer as an interruption to your work; serving the customer is the central part of your job.

2. **See things from the customer's perspective.**
   - Try to understand how your customer feels about things and develop the habit of looking at every interaction from their point of view.

   > **TOP TIP**
   > If you don't take care of your customer, your customer will find someone else who will.

   - Remember that you will never know your client completely. Don't make assumptions, as customers' reactions are very difficult to predict.

3. **Be available.**
   - Never forget that customers are people who want attention and recognition, so be there for them.
   - Make contacting you easy. Give out your email and telephone details and decide with your customer how communications should be handled.
   - Set up a system (voicemail and email) to ensure all messages get through to you. Always return calls as soon as possible.

   > **TOP TIP**
   > The most important time to be available for your client is when there is a problem. Don't ignore the problem – instead, make the call and face the situation. Not facing up to a problem is unacceptable and will not be forgotten.

4. **Seek to understand and to be understood.**
   - Make sure you both have a common understanding of everything you discuss, as absolutely anything can be misunderstood and most problems arise because of miscommunication.
   - Seek to understand by asking questions and paraphrasing comments made. Seek to be understood by repeating what you are saying and asking customers what they have understood you to mean.

5. **Be reliable.**

- Act on anything you agree to do (e.g. if you are asked for something, get it immediately and if you are asked to do something, follow through when you say you will).
- Manage the customer's expectations. It impresses no one to say you'll do something quickly and then fail to deliver. If you can't do or get something immediately, just explain why and indicate when it will be done.
- Never tell the customer something that you don't believe. If the client can't trust you, the relationship will not last.

6. **Be positive.**

- Adopt a can-do attitude. Focus on what you can do to help, not what you can't.
- Be upbeat in your dealings with customers; this does not mean that you should agree with everything they say, it just means that any negative response should be managed.

CHECK LIST Say & Don't Say

✓ I don't know but I'll find out.	✗ I don't know.
✓ What I can do is...	✗ I'm not allowed to do that.
✓ This is who can help.	✗ That's not my job.
✓ I understand your frustration.	✗ You're right – this stinks.
✓ Let's see what we can do about this.	✗ That's not my fault.
✓ It will be difficult but I'll try my best.	✗ You want it by when?
✓ I'm sorry.	✗ Calm down.
✓ I'll be with you in just a moment.	✗ I'm busy right now.
✓ I'll call you back.	✗ Call me back.

7. **Go the extra mile.**

- Aim to treat the customer even better than they expect to be treated. Take the initiative to rectify potential issues and ensure they are always happy with your service.

8. **Show customers you like them (even if you don't).**

- Get to know your customers personally. Treat them well and show an interest in them.
- Show them you care about them and that you will do your best to keep them happy.
- Greet them with a smile. Be happy on the phone, it will come across in your voice.
- Make sure they have an enjoyable experience dealing with you; when it comes down to it, clients stay or leave based on personal relationships.

TOP TIP

How formal or informal your relationship with your client is, depends on your respective positions:
- If you are at the same level, you can become informal more quickly (e.g. calling each other by first names).
- If your client is more senior than you, you should adopt the level of formality dictated by the client.

9. **Be professional.**

- Be a good ambassador for your company. Speak well of your company and be sensitive and discreet in times of trouble. Never forget that you are not obliged to divulge any information, even if a probing question is posed directly.
- Never share problems about yourself or your firm, no matter how friendly you become. People respect loyalty. If you don't like something about the company, talk to somebody internal about it, never someone external.

TOP TIP

Keep informed about what is going on in your company and in your client's company to avoid embarrassment at being told something you should already have known.

10. **Never take your customers for granted.**

- People notice when they are made feel wanted and special and when they are not. Customers do not appreciate getting special treatment when you are looking for their business and then being forgotten about when you have got it.
- Work at keeping your clients. After all, a customer you have is more valuable than one you are trying to woo.

Customer complaints

Complaints are often seen as something negative, as something you don't want to receive, but nothing could be further from the truth. Of course, someone yelling abuse at you about the awful service they've received is not very nice, but complaints are essential to giving good customer service:

- Without complaints, you will never know what areas are offending customers and perhaps causing you to lose business.
  - No matter how good a service you provide, it will never be perfect.
- Sorting out complaints not only turns negative situations around, converting an irate customer into a happy loyal one, but it also prevents the person badmouthing about their experience to others.
- Sorting out complaints should improve service in general.
  - If the bad service offended one person, it will probably have offended others as well.

TOP TIP
If people are dissatisfied with your service, they will tell someone; aim to be that someone.

To keep improving, you should actively encourage feedback from your clients about what they like and the improvements that they would like to see. Complaints are only useful if they are acted upon. Don't waste your time soliciting complaints if you are not prepared to work at rectifying the causes. Most people don't like complaining, so make it easy for them.

CHECK LIST
Make complaining easy by:
- ✓ Letting customers know that complaints are welcome.
- ✓ Giving lots of opportunities (by phone, in writing and in person) for feedback to come through.
- ✓ Asking people what they think.
- ✓ Being approachable. People tend to want to give companies they like a second chance and are more likely to complain to get problems sorted out.
- ✓ Making changes (made due to a complaint) visible; many people don't make complaints as they think it will have no impact.

Handling complaints properly

The customer is not always right but they will not be your customer for long if you tell them they are wrong. The trick with complaining customers is to make them feel that they have made a valid point and that you are taking it on board and will do something about it. The emphasis should be on solving the problem, not assigning blame. Making even a small gesture will make your customer feel as though you are conceding something and they are gaining something.

1. **Let people vent their annoyance.**

   - Make your customer feel that they are being listened to. Often people need to get everything off their chest before they can begin to accept a solution. For 80% of the time, all people want is to vent their frustrations and get an apology and an acceptable explanation.

   - End the conversation politely and offer to call back if the customer is excessively rude and hostile. Calmly let it be known that your company values business but insists on civility.

CHECK LIST Dos and Don'ts

✓ Open your ears and close your mouth; the customer's views count, not yours.	✗ Don't jump into resolving the issue.
✓ Listen to how they describe the problem.	✗ Don't start to justify your actions.
✓ Remain calm and courteous even if your customer is rude or unpleasant.	✗ Don't argue.
✓ Give the customer the benefit of the doubt; assume he/she is telling the truth.	✗ Don't take abuse from a customer, no matter how important he/she is.

TOP TIP

When people are angry they tend to speak loudly. It is a natural response to speak back at the same volume, but don't! Reply in a calm, controlled manner and gradually the person complaining will adjust down to your volume.

---

2. **Express regret.**

   - Let the customer know that you understand how they feel and that you care about what they are saying (e.g. 'I see what you mean').

   - Don't be afraid to empathize. Empathizing with your customer does not mean that you are admitting liability (which may be important from a legal perspective).

3. **Accept responsibility for the problem.**

- Understand that once the customer has complained to you, you are responsible for resolving the problem, irrespective of who is to blame.
- Pass the complaint directly to the person best placed to resolve it, if it is so serious that you are unable to resolve it. Don't waste time dealing with people who don't have the power to rectify matters; nothing is more annoying for a customer with a complaint than to be passed from one person to another in an attempt to address it.

TOP TIP

Even if someone else takes responsibility for a complaint, you should (as good service to the customer who complained to you) keep track of the situation until the customer is satisfied with the outcome.

4. **Work together to find a solution.**

- Consult the customer to find out how they would like to resolve the problem. Remember that customers may well ask for more than they expect to get, so be prepared to get them to be more reasonable.
- Offer the customer some choices if they don't know how they would like the problem resolved.
- Never push a solution on a customer; if the customer is not happy with the outcome, you still have a problem needing a resolution.

5. **Settle the complaint quickly.**

- Keep the time it takes to resolve a problem to a minimum; the longer it takes, the more annoyed the customer will be and the more likely he/she will be to complain to others, giving your company a bad reputation.

TOP TIP

Keep customers informed about what is happening with their complaint. They will be happier, even if it takes longer to resolve.

6. **Follow up.**

- Take time to go back to the customer a few weeks later to see if the customer is happy with everything. He/she won't forget your concern.

Client knowledge

Having a good understanding of what your customer really wants allows you to cater for them in an appropriate manner. The more customized a service you can offer, the better relationship you will establish and the more likely your customer is to remain with you. Yet, people usually serve their customers based on assumptions about what the customer wants. These assumptions tend to be formed over time and are rarely based on hard data. It is therefore not surprising that these assumptions are often wrong.

TOP TIP
Remember that your smallest customer today could be your biggest tomorrow.

The only way truly to understand what a customer wants is to ask them directly. Sometimes they don't really know, or do know but can't translate it into practical terms. In order to understand what might be useful, you need to collect data to create a complete picture of the customer. With this information, you'll get a clear idea of who your top clients are and who is more hassle than they are worth.

CHECK LIST

Build a file containing the following information:

✓ **Buying behaviour**
- What do they buy and how often do they buy it?
- Do they pay on time, or very late?
- Do they need a lot of after sales service? How much does this cost you? Is the cost of giving service to the customer greater than the reward?

✓ **People**
- How do they make decisions?
- Who has ultimate responsibility?
- What kind of person are they? Do they like facts or do they work instinctively?

✓ **Value**
- What is their value (both current and potential) to you? What revenue would you lose if you lost the customer? What future revenue do you think they could generate?
- Why are they valuable to you? What profit do they generate? What credibility do they give your business?

TOP TIP
You can never know too much about your customers.

Client entertainment

Client entertainment is becoming increasingly common as competition intensifies and relationship building is seen as a key to success. The most common forms of entertainment are business lunches and dinners, drinks and hospitality events. Client entertainment can seem glamorous at first, but after a while, you will probably wonder:

Do you have to go?

- Go on corporate trips or to sports events and concerts if you are invited, unless you have a good reason not to.
- Speak to your boss if you are being asked to go to a lot of events outside of working hours and they start to infringe on your life outside work. Be reasonable but firm with your boss (e.g. agree to go out two evenings a week and only one Friday a month).

Should you drink?

- Have a drink if you like, but limit your intake, irrespective of what others do. It is important that you enjoy the event, as it is hard for guests to enjoy themselves if the host is too uptight.

> **MORE INFO?**
> See p. 182 for more on cultivating a balanced lifestyle and p. 153 for how to say no to your boss.

- Be responsible for your guests. Don't ply them with alcohol. If they have a lot to drink, organize a taxi but don't make a fuss.

> **MORE INFO?**
> See p. 179 for more on drinking at office parties.

What should you talk about?

- Keep business talk to a minimum.

> **MORE INFO?**
> See p. 8 for more on making small talk and p. 51 surviving business lunches.

What should you wear?

- Make sure you find out the dress code (e.g. is it black tie or smart casual?).
- Make sure your guest knows the dress code as well.

Being a customer

> **TOP TIP**
> Always get the name of the person you are dealing with. It will make you more credible if you have to call up again and may prevent you from having to explain a whole situation again if you can speak to them. It also makes the person giving their name more responsible.

1. **Get people on your side.**
   - Build a relationship. People are more likely to help you if you treat them as allies rather than enemies, so even if they fail to deliver, stay calm and show that you understand their position.

2. **Be polite but firm.**
   - Always be friendly but professional.
   - Demand good service but don't act like a prima donna.
   - Don't get aggressive with people as it makes them defensive. If you have a problem, see how you could help the situation instead of bawling at someone about how dissatisfied you are. Don't, however, take the responsibility away from them; ask them what they recommend and stand up for yourself by calmly expressing your disappointment at the situation.

3. **Know and ask for what you want.**
   - Don't expect people to know what you want. The clearer you are about what you want and the better you communicate it, the more likely you are to get it.

4. **Mutually agree what you want.**
   - Make sure people understand what you want and get their buy in and commitment to get it for you. Always get this commitment (be it on dates, prices or penalties) in writing and make someone accept responsibility for your service.

12

Managing yourself

➡ Career planning

➡ Self-marketing

➡ Office politics and social events

➡ Cultivating a balanced lifestyle

Excellent careers do not happen by accident, nor do they happen if they are left to someone else to take care of. If you want to succeed, you must actively manage your career. You need to ensure that you are on the right career path and take care of yourself so that you stay healthy and sane. To do this, you need to have a good understanding of what you are like, what is important to you and what you want to get from life. This chapter will make you think about your career, as well as providing advice on building your own brand, dealing with office politics, attending office parties, minimizing stress and managing your time.

Career planning

It is very easy to get caught up in the day-to-day activities of your job and lose sight of the bigger picture – your career. If you just focus on your job, you will probably wake up some day realizing that you are nowhere near achieving your dreams. To prevent this from happening, you need to think through your career plans, periodically review them and take control of making them happen.

 CHECK LIST Your Career Plan

Take a blank page and jot down your answers to the following questions. Keep them somewhere safe so that you can revisit them.
- ✓ Where are you now? (Your role and responsibilities)
- ✓ Where do you want to be in 5 years' time?
- ✓ Who is currently in the position you aspire to?
- ✓ Why do you want to be in that role?
  - By naming the aspects of the job you get a good idea of what is important to you. As time passes and your priorities change, you can easily identify which aspects are still important to you.
- ✓ What do you need to do to be in that position? Be specific.
  - What knowledge do you need?
  - What skills do you need?
  - What experience do you need?
  - What are the company guidelines?
- ✓ How are you going to achieve the above?
  - What training courses could you attend?
  - What responsibilities should you try to get?
  - What books should you read?

While everyone needs goals to have direction in life, it is important not to become imprisoned by them. Use your goals to guide you but remain flexible and patient as success takes time and opportunities often come from unusual places.

 TOP TIP
Think big. The only thing that can hold you back is yourself.

 TOP TIP
Keep adapting; things change whether or not you want them to.

Making it happen

You and you alone are responsible for your career, so make sure that you take full control over the choices you make and the jobs you do.

1. **Find the right job. There must always be a reason for being in the position you are in. You need to rethink your position if your job does not include one of the following:**
   - You are developing a skill base and/or gaining experience you need.
   - You are on a path that takes you to the position you want to be in.
   - You are making important contacts.
   - You are earning enough money to enable you to keep afloat at a later stage while you work on another project.

2. **Develop your skills. The early years of your career are absolutely essential for experimenting and learning new skills.**
   - Break out of your comfort zone and work on improving your weak spots instead of focusing on your strengths (which is rewarding in the short term). You may not appear to be as impressive an employee as you could, but over time you will have built a set of all-round skills that will stand you in good stead in the future.
   - Never stop learning. At some point in your career, the time will come to work in a job that requires you to do what you do best, but you should keep updating your skills.

3. **Seek guidance. There are many people who can help you, so don't be shy about approaching them for advice.**
   - Company mentors (either formally or informally).
   - Someone who is in a position similar to one you would like.
   - Professional career advisers.
   - Friends (people who know you well often have very good opinions on what you would be good at, often things you don't see yourself).

4. **Get promoted.**
   - Find out if your company has a set of guidelines for promotion. If they do, make sure that you do what is required. Document your activities and use these as support during promotion discussions.
   - Find out who decides your promotion and have a chat with them well before any promotion rounds. Encourage them to be honest and specific about what you need to do. Work on the suggested areas for improvement.
   - Market yourself (see section on Self-marketing).

Areas for personal development

Try to see everything as an opportunity to widen and deepen your experience. Some of the best lessons are learned by making mistakes, so don't be afraid to make them. Of course, there is no end to the training that you could go on, or the things you could learn. To simplify matters, consider these five areas for development:

1. **Your knowledge.**
   - General (Do you know what is going on in the world?)
   - Industry (Have you a clear understanding of what your particular industry is like, e.g. size of the market, key players, trends, main issues?)
   - Functions (Do you know how the main departments in your company work in general, and how your area or department works in particular?)

2. **Your know-how.**
   - Computer skills
   - Research skills
   - Language skills

3. **Your cognitive ability.**
   - Problem solving
   - Analytical ability
   - Decision making
   - Planning and delegation of work

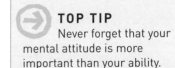

TOP TIP
Never forget that your mental attitude is more important than your ability.

4. **Your people skills.**
   - Communication skills
   - Empathy with others
   - Ability to influence
   - Networking skills

5. **Your attitude.**
   - Confidence (Do you believe in yourself?)
   - Positivity (Have you a can-do attitude?)
   - Proactive (Are you a self-starter?)
   - Resilience (Are you both emotionally and intellectually strong?)
   - Flexiblility (Are you open-minded and open to change?)
   - Focus (Do you work with the end in mind?)
   - Vision (Do you see the big picture?)

Self-marketing

People, like products, have a 'brand image'. This image is usually the result of how others perceive the person to be, irrespective of what that person is actually like. People constantly 'judge books by their covers' and often form extremely strong views on others based on very little information and interaction. You can, however, control how you are perceived to a certain degree so it's worthwhile learning how best to market yourself.

1. **Think of yourself as a product.**
   - Decide what characteristics you want your product to have.
   - Try to find out what your 'brand image' is by asking your boss at appraisal sessions, or informally asking colleagues.
   - Be clear about the image you want to project and if people are seeing another one, make the appropriate changes. This is not about being fake or superficial; it is about actively boosting a certain image of you.

> **TOP TIP**
> Don't worry too much if you haven't figured out what your brand is yet – your late twenties and early thirties are for discovering that.

2. **Identify your market.**
   - Think about whom you should market yourself to (e.g. your boss, colleagues, peers, clients and senior people in your company).

> **TOP TIP**
> Never waste face-time with senior people. Keep them informed about what you are doing. Be positive and upbeat (this is not the time to moan).

3. **Actively market yourself.**
   - Don't feel bad about marketing yourself. If you don't, no one else will. Just be careful that you do it in a controlled, non-aggressive way.
   - Be able to explain what you are working on clearly and precisely in 30 seconds (this is often known as the 'Elevator Test').
   - Keep your brand image consistent; like all products, you cannot be all things to all people.

Building your brand

There is no point in marketing a product if the product can't live up to the hype. Self-marketing is not about bragging, there must be some substance behind it, so make sure you:

1. **Become competent at your job.**
   - Work hard to be the best at what you do and learn from your mistakes.
   - Get a good grasp of the basics of your job (be they technical or creative).
   - Focus on things that matter and get results.
   - Check your work thoroughly and deliver on time.
   - Try to add value. You add value when you find better ways to do your job.
   - Never leave work unfinished.

2. **Have confidence in yourself.**
   - Be self-assured but never arrogant.
   - Walk with a purpose.
   - Focus on what you can do, not what you can't.
   - Express yourself with confidence.
   - Ask when you are not sure of something.
   - Accept praise without embarrassment and give credit to others, where due.

3. **Show empathy towards others.**
   - Treat others as you would like to be treated.
   - Be approachable and show you care.

TOP TIP
Don't depend on approval from others.

4. **Demonstrate personal integrity.**
   - Be totally trustworthy.
   - Always speak the truth diplomatically.
   - Be loyal to your company, boss and colleagues (especially if absent).

MIND YOUR MANNERS!
Never spread rumours about others, tell on a colleague or badmouth colleagues and the company you work for – it is unprofessional and you'll just end up making yourself look bad.

5. **Have a positive disposition.**
   - Smile when you meet people.
   - Learn to laugh.
   - Adopt a 'can-do' attitude.
   - Approach problems with solutions in mind.

TOP TIP
Don't say, 'I don't know'. Say, 'I don't know but I'll find out.'

6. **Look the part.**

- Dress appropriately. The image you create of yourself sends out a powerful message about how you perceive yourself and how you expect to be treated.
- Try to strike a balance between conformity and individuality.
- Find someone you respect and use that person as a benchmark if you are not sure what to wear. Remember that it is safer to be too formal than not formal enough.
- Dress in a way that will make clients feel comfortable (e.g. do they want you to look creative or reliable?).

 CHECK LIST

You don't need to spend a lot of money, just try to look:

✓ **Smart**
- Invest in one classic suit.
- Avoid wearing jeans, leggings, tracksuits or big woolly jumpers (i.e. anything that you would wear if you were lazing around at home).
- Avoid wearing t-shirts or sweatshirts with slogans or statements.
- Avoid wearing humorous ties or cufflinks.

✓ **Elegant**
- Stick to classic colours (e.g. black, white, navy, brown, camel).
- Keep patterns to a minimum.
- Keep jewellery to a minimum.

✓ **Together**
- Handbags/briefcases should not be scuffed or stuffed with rubbish.
- Glasses should be suitably discreet and kept clean.
- Diaries should be as sleek as possible. Avoid stuffing them with paper.
- Consider investing in a good pen rather than using cheap biros.

✓ **Groomed**
- Hair should be clean, neat and cut regularly.
- Nails should be clean, cut and not overly manicured. If you wear nail varnish, keep it subtle.
- Makeup should be kept to a minimum.
- Perfume or aftershave should smell fresh and clean but not overpowering.

Office politics and social events

Office politics and social events are important aspects of working in a company. They can also be the source of much stress, as people often do not know how they should behave. The following pages should help you to navigate successfully through any occasion, be it an office party or a politicized meeting.

Managing office politics

Much could be said about office politics, but the following three things are the most important:

1. **It exists.**

   Like it or not, office politics is a part of company life. It is a fact of life that any large group of people will have some element of political activity within it. The political game is intensified in companies where every employee has his/her own career plan and every group and department have their own personal agenda.

2. **It is not necessarily dirty.**

   Office politics tends to have very negative connotations. Office politics, the business of influencing and persuading, is negative when it is used in an unacceptable or unethical way for self-interest and personal gain. However, it can also be positive. Politics can be used to influence others in an informal manner to achieve goals that are for the good of the organization.

3. **It can make or break you.**

   You are not an island; you depend on others to get your job done. As you have to interact with others (who will have their own personal agendas), you will have to deal with the politicking that goes with it. Although rarely discussed, political skills are probably one of the most important skills in determining job success. If you are not aware of the politics that exist at work, it will affect how successful you are.

   > **TOP TIP**
   > Avoid negative politics. Don't get a reputation as a political animal unless it is a positive one.

Skills to survive office politics

Although you have a natural level of political awareness, there is a lot that can be done to improve your political skills. The first step is to recognize the politics at play all around you. Once you have done that, you should make an effort to be:

Informed

- Know where the power lies and how to get access to it.
- Know what is going on in the company (not just your department).

Perceptive

- Try to understand others' aspirations and motivations.
- Think how people will react in situations.

TOP TIP
Keep your ears open and your mouth shut.

Persuasive

- Hone your communication skills (spoken and written).
- Learn to influence others. Remember what Aristotle said: 'The fool tells me his reasons. The wise man persuades me with my own.'
- Know your own power. Think about how much influence you have over your boss and colleagues.

Assertive

- Be strong-willed when necessary.
- Look after yourself. You're all you've got.

Diplomatic

- Never offend anyone.
- Have a win/win disposition.
- Give in to others' demands when necessary.

TOP TIP
Never assume anything.

Flexible

- Expect change. In the world of politics nothing is permanent. Friends become enemies, and foes become friends.

Wary

- Be careful whom you trust.
- Don't open up too soon.
- Watch out for people you threaten.

Principled

- Value your own judgements and trust your instincts. If it feels wrong, it usually *is* wrong and no one achieves long-term success by being dishonest or underhand.

Crying in the office

There is an unwritten rule that you should avoid crying at work and despite improvements in equality of the sexes, it is still much more unacceptable for a man to cry. However, don't worry if you do; crying is not all that uncommon.

If you can, try to stop the tears by:

- Breathing deeply through your nose and exhaling through your mouth.
- Distracting yourself by drinking ice-cold water or pinching your armpit.
- Looking up to drain the tears back into the ducts.

If you still think you are going to cry:

- Head straight for the toilet. Don't run, just walk calmly and keep your tears in until you get there. Have a good, quiet cry in one of the cubicles. It is better to release your emotion as it will come out sooner or later and it is best not done in front of other people.
- Splash your face with cool water when you have finished. Go outside to get some fresh air if you are particularly upset. When you are feeling composed, go back to your desk.
- Thank your colleagues for their understanding if you have started to cry in front of them and then get on with your work. Avoid entering into conversations with co-workers about what has upset you.

Office parties and social events

Go, even if you don't want to

- Put in an appearance, even for a short while.
- Find out who will be there and think through things you need to discuss with them. As long as it is appropriate, this is a good time to have a chat.
- Eat something before you go. Don't stuff your face with food there.
- Don't bring someone uninvited.
- Treat your 'significant other' well if invited. How you treat your partner will reflect on you.

Move around

- Don't spend the night talking to the people you already know. This is a great opportunity to meet people.
- Smile and look like you are enjoying yourself.
- Don't ignore your boss; engage in conversation, even for a short while. Don't monopolize your boss for the night either, as he/she will want to mingle.

 TOP TIP
Remain standing (it makes you more approachable) but don't hover around the buffet table all night.

Introduce people

- Introduce yourself to people you don't know. Wear your name badge if one is provided.
- Introduce people if you think they don't know each other.
- If your boss forgets to introduce you and has introduced everyone else, cheerfully introduce yourself (e.g. 'And I'm Paul Jones. I work with Mr Lee').

Keep topics light and safe

- Be loyal to your boss, colleagues and company.
- Don't get too personal and don't divulge confidences.
- Don't talk or complain about work (especially to your boss).
- Don't monopolize conversations or talk about yourself too much.
- Never ask colleagues something that might make them feel uncomfortable (e.g. why they are not drinking or why they are leaving).
- Move away from people who want to complain or gossip.

MORE INFO?

See p.6 for more on making introductions.

Remain professional

- Remember your position when talking to superiors.
- Avoid being too friendly.
- Avoid flirting.
- Wear appropriate clothing.

MIND YOUR MANNERS!

Never remind people of what they said or did.

Stay sober

- Know your limits and stick well within them. This is not the time to avail yourself of 'free drink'.
- Drink what you usually drink; this is not the time to experiment.
- Switch to water if you start to feel light-headed. If you feel ill, excuse yourself and leave quietly.
- Never apologize for not drinking alcohol but do be decisive about what you want (e.g. 'I'll have a Pelligrino' sounds a lot more savvy than 'Oh, I'll just have a glass of water').

Try not to be the first or last to leave

- Thank the person who organized the event before you leave.
- Be careful with whom you leave, people love to gossip.

TOP TIP

If you do something that you regret, don't pretend it never happened. Apologize profusely as soon as possible but don't dwell on it, move on and learn from the experience.

Office relationships

Given how much time people spend at work, it is very common for two people who work together to become attracted to each other. Although most of us are ruled by our hearts not our heads when it comes to relationships, some thought is required, given the potential repercussions of an office romance. Try to:

Assess the seriousness of the relationship

- Give it a week or two to see if it is more than just a fling. Be extremely discreet during this time so that people don't suspect anything. Avoid arriving and leaving work together, having lunch together and spending a lot of time at each other's desk.
- Find out what your company policy is, if it is a more serious relationship. Often people are not allowed to date people in their team or department and may need to move to another team or department.

Let people know about it as naturally as possible

- Speak to your boss or head of department privately and let them know if it is to become public knowledge.
- Try to let people know as naturally as possible so that it is not a big announcement.

Avoid public displays of affection

- Don't engage in any sexual interaction in the workplace under any circumstances.

Keep problems out of work

- Conduct the relationship with maturity.

Stay on top of your work

- Don't let it affect your work.
- Think through the implications the relationship will have on your job and relationship with colleagues (especially if you are dating your boss).
- Don't spend every moment together.
- Be completely equitable in work issues that involve your partner.

TOP TIP

Whether it is a fling or a serious long-term relationship, you should conduct your relationship discreetly.

The office grapevine

The office grapevine is an informal network where information is shared and often embellished. Anyone can participate in the grapevine but it tends to exist between people who get on well.

Get hooked into it

- Find out who tends to get wind of 'inside information' and plug into their communication lines. While you should not get too involved in the office grapevine, keeping your ear to the ground is generally a good idea.

Be responsible with the information

- Inform the appropriate person about what is being said if there are negative, harmful or incorrect rumours circulating about them, so that action may be taken to dispel the rumours. Be careful how you do this, you don't want to get too involved.

Be careful whom you trust

- Never expect to have a truly private conversation; few people keep their word of not telling others.

> **TOP TIP**
> Never trust someone who tells you something that was told in confidence; you may be next to have your private life broadcast.

Don't believe everything you hear

- Think twice before taking action based on such information, the grapevine is often the source of rumours and incorrect information.

Don't get involved in negative gossiping

- Acknowledge that a certain amount of gossiping is part of working life but try to steer clear of the malicious and spiteful type.
- Try to limit personal conversations during business hours.

> **TOP TIP**
> If you show others that you are not interested in gossip and you defend absent people when you hear them being badmouthed, you may be cut out of the gossip ring and made to feel isolated. However, in the long run, you will command more respect and people will be more likely to trust and admire you.

Cultivating a balanced lifestyle

Too many people get caught up in the stresses and strains of their job and begins to dominate their lives. Remember that work is only one part (albeit an important part) of your whole life; relationships, friends, family, time for oneself, hobbies, and fun are equally important. If you neglect these important areas, life begins to lose its meaning and you become frustrated and unfulfilled. Having a balanced life is much easier said than done and requires a lot of hard work, but cultivating one is necessary for long-term success.

TOP TIP
Keep work and home separate; don't bring work home.

The following are ways to help you control your work/life balance:

Simplify your life

- Know what is important to you and focus on that.
- Dispense with activities that complicate your life and stress you.

Organize yourself

- Set up direct debit accounts to pay all your bills.
- Set aside time to do domestic chores or, if you can afford it, hire domestic help for a couple of hours a week. It is amazing how out of control people feel when work at home starts to pile up.

MORE INFO?
See p. 153 for more on how to say no.

Lay down some rules

- Sit down with your boss and discuss your working style. Stress that you are dedicated to the job but that you also need to keep a balance in your life outside work. Agree to make at least one day of the weekend (but preferably both Saturday and Sunday) off limits and discuss how late you are expected to stay at work.

Say no!

- Don't be afraid to say no if someone asks you to do something and you cannot give him/her the energy (emotional or physical), time or brain power. Recognize how much pressure you put yourself under when you say yes every time you're asked to do something.

Never spend as much as you earn

- Keep control by saving some money. It is much easier to spend less than it is to earn more.

Take care of your body

- See next section.

Use your time well

- See section on time management.

Taking care of yourself

When you are working very hard it is difficult to take care of yourself properly. Often people are in either a virtuous or a vicious spiral of doing all (eating sensibly, going to the gym and getting a good night's sleep) or nothing (junk food, no exercise and little sleep). Discipline and routine are essential to stay balanced and healthy on a regular basis. Even if you do have relapses, keep striving for a healthier lifestyle:

Food

- Never skip meals. Even if you are busy, make time to eat. If you feel you haven't got the time, ask someone to bring something back for you when they go out.
- Minimize the amount of convenience and processed foods you eat. They are low in vitamins, nutrients and energy.

CHECK LIST

Try to eat healthily:
- ✓ *Breakfast:* Eat fresh fruit every other day.
- ✓ *Lunch:* Swap sandwiches for soup, sushi, salads or noodles.
- ✓ *Snacks:* Swap crisps and chocolate for dried fruit and nuts.
- ✓ *Dinner:* Eat your dinner at least two hours before you go to bed.

Drink

- Drink 1.5 litres of filtered or bottled water every day.
- Cut down on tea and coffee.

Exercise

- Try to get 30 minutes of cardiovascular exercise, three times a week.
- Climb the stairs rather than take the lift and walk rather than take a cab.

TOP TIP
Take a quick 5 minute walk every evening when you get home. It will clear your mind, stretch your legs, get some clean air into your lungs and help you sleep.

Relaxation

- Do something that you enjoy that relaxes you.
- Try yoga if you suffer from stress.

Sleep

- Try to get as much sleep as you need (7 hours is recommended).
- Try to go to bed and wake up at the same time every day, even weekends.

Stress management

At some point during your working life, you'll become stressed. How often and how much you get stressed depends entirely on you, as stress is your personal response to pressure. The pressure may be an outside source but it may also come from within. As stress can severely affect your mental and physical wellbeing, it should not be ignored. There are many ways you can deal with stress:

Put things in perspective

- Imagine how bad the situation could be. Don't waste your time being stressed about things that, in the grand scheme of things, are not that important.
- Tell yourself all that is positive in your life. Making a list helps.
- Take things day by day. Rein in your thoughts and don't worry about what lies way off in the future.
- Imagine yourself a year from now. How will the issue that is causing you so much worry seem then? Will you even be able to remember it?

Escape for a while

- Take a coffee break.
- Read a magazine or a newspaper for a while.
- Go for a walk in a nearby park and have a good yell or a good cry. Get it all out of your system.
- Go to the bathroom and sit in the cubicle and meditate for 5 minutes.

> **TOP TIP**
> Close your eyes and focus on your breathing. Start with your toes and work your way up to your head, relaxing each muscle one by one. Enjoy the serenity and when you are feeling calm, open your eyes, stand up, stretch and feel positive about what you have to do.

Be positive

- Concentrate on what you can do and do it, rather than wallowing in how bad things are. You can always do something, no matter how dreadful the situation is. Good and bad situations are really just a state of mind.
- Ask someone to help you. It may be all that is needed.
- Tidy your desk, clear your clutter or write a list of everything you need to do. It can help you feel more in control.
- Visualize everything working out.

Treat yourself to something nice

- Accept that you will not always feel great or do the right thing. Don't beat yourself up for not being perfect.
- Think of how you would try to cheer up a friend who was down and be your own best friend.
- Make a list of all the things that you like that make you feel good (e.g. a nice massage or a long bath) and when you are low pick one or two of them and treat yourself.

TOP TIP
Do something fun. Rent a funny film, go to a comedy, read a funny book or have some friends around for a good giggle. Don't underestimate the power of laughter.

Proactively work to reduce stress

- Try to work out what triggers your stress. Keep a diary and try to work out what gets you worked up. Once you understand the triggers, you can take steps to manage the stress.
- Remember that the only person you can change is yourself, so if it is your boss or a colleague that gets you worked up, you need to change how *you* react to them.
- Learn to understand your stress personality as often it's not the stress itself that's the problem, but how you respond to it.

CHECK LIST
Try to understand your stress personality:
- ✓ If you behave like an ostrich and refuse to acknowledge there is a problem until it gets the better of you:
  - Try to become more aware of how you feel by keeping a diary.
  - Look for someone that you can confide in (a counsellor may be a good idea).
- ✓ If you appear cool and collected in a crisis despite crumbling inside:
  - Learn to say no to the demands of others as they don't realize how you feel.
  - Do some exercise to give your feelings an outlet for release.
- ✓ If you react to stress by becoming snappy and irritable:
  - Learn some relaxation techniques.
  - Try to accept that it is OK not to be perfect.
- ✓ If you explode like a volcano:
  - Learn ways to keep calm (e.g. counting to ten or deep-breathing).
  - Avoid stimulants such as caffeine, chocolate, tea, cola and sugar.

Stress-free travel

Increasingly, people have to travel abroad for their job. It can be exciting but can also be quite stressful and can take a lot out of you, but there are some things you can do to make things easier for yourself.

Make sure you have packed all the essentials

CHECK LIST

✓ PMT (passport, money, tickets).

✓ Credit cards.

✓ Trip information (your itinerary, the names and numbers of everyone you are going to see and directions to destination).

✓ Toiletries (especially toothbrush and shaving kit).

✓ An extra shirt/top, set of underwear and socks/tights – just in case you need to stay an extra day.

Get to the airport on time

- Book a cab with a reliable company to take you to the airport.
- Start tidying up work sooner than you think you should.
- Give yourself plenty of time to get to the airport.

Dress appropriately

- Wear your most comfortable suit or outfit. If possible, choose something made from natural fabrics that is warm and doesn't crease.
- Keep your hair clean and tied back (to avoid static build up) and don't wear much make-up.

Take carry-on luggage only

- Invest in a good bag with wheels and small enough to be considered hand luggage.
- Pack as lightly as possible.
- Put all cosmetics/toiletries in plastic bags to prevent spillage over your clothes.

TOP TIP

Treat all flight attendants with respect. If you start getting annoyed, you just get yourself stressed.

Booking long-haul flights

Take extra care when booking long-haul flights as travelling at different times or sitting in different parts of the plane can make a big difference. If you:

Want to sleep on the plane:

- Book a flight that will get you to your destination in the morning time.
- Book a window seat so that you can sleep without disturbance.

> **TOP TIP**
> Set up meetings for when you will be most alert (i.e. from your time zone).

Have difficulty sleeping:

- Book a flight that will get you to your destination in the evening.
- Book an aisle seat so you can move about.

Don't like flying:

- Try to get a seat that is over the wing (it's the most stable part).

Need extra legroom:

- Ask for a seat in the emergency exit row or in a bulkhead seat (the front row of each cabin).

Avoiding flight-related problems

Time zone

- Adopt the time zone you are travelling to when you get on the flight.

Sleeping

- Don't sleep longer than usual when you arrive.

Drinking

- Drink lots of water.
- Avoid caffeine and alcohol as they will dehydrate you.

Eating

- Try to eat something before you fly, rather than eating the plane food.
- Eat lightly.

Exercise

- Move about, don't stay in your seat for the entire flight.
- Go for a brisk walk (if it is daylight) when you arrive.

> **TOP TIP**
> Just because you are away from home doesn't mean you should stop living. Do something to unwind after work: go to the gym, the cinema, meet up with friends or colleagues for dinner or go to bed with a good book.

Time management

One of the best ways of reducing stress and creating a balanced lifestyle is to learn good time management. You are responsible for the quality of your time so make every minute count.

Understand how you use your time

- Know when you are most productive and unproductive and schedule your activities to match your productivity (e.g. tidy your desk last thing at night when you are feeling tired, rather than first thing in the morning when your alert brain could be put to better use).
- Identify all of your roles (employee, family, member of a team or association) and the amount of time each requires.

Plan what you need to do

- Make a weekly plan of action and be realistic about what you can achieve. Spreading things out over a week gives you flexibility.

TOP TIP
Think in the morning, act after lunch.

TOP TIP
Write a 'To Do' list every evening before you leave work, when what you have to do the following day is clear in your mind. Similarly, every Friday, think through what you need to achieve the following week.

Prioritize your work

- Learn to separate the important and urgent from the trivial.
- Look at each task and decide whether it is a 'Must do', 'Should do' or 'Nice to do' task. All 'Must do' items should be completed first (don't do little tasks 'just to get them out of the way'). 'Nice to do' items should only be completed once everything else has been done.

Draw up a schedule

- Give yourself blocks of time when you can work uninterrupted.
- Include breaks in your schedule – you should have a lunch break even if it is just a quick one.
- Keep your timetable flexible as the unexpected usually occurs.

TOP TIP
Focus on the things that count.

TOP TIP
Remember, everything takes longer than you think.

Get what you planned done

- Start somewhere; the longer you put something off, the harder it is to do it.
- Work with the end in mind. Always think what you're trying to achieve.
- Get ahead and stay ahead. Get in the habit of starting work when you get it and finishing it ahead of time. Leaving things until the last minute causes unnecessary stress and anxiety.
- Delegate tasks where you are not really adding a lot of value.
- Learn to say 'no' to other people's unreasonable requests.
- Group small tasks (e.g. responding to and making phone calls and emails) together and do them when your energy is low.
- Ask yourself 'Is this the best use of my time now?'

Time savers

1. **Keep a good system.**

TOP TIP
Start work half an hour early.

   - Have a good diary with all your meetings, appointments and commitments as well as your 'To Do' list.
   - Keep all contacts in an easily accessible format.

2. **Organize your files.**
   - Set up easy-to-access files for all of your information.
   - Be ruthless about what you keep.
   - Every month, set aside 15 minutes to eliminate non-essential material.

3. **Handle each piece of paper once.**
   - Act on it immediately.
   - Pass it on to someone else if it is more appropriate that they deal with it. Don't do this to shirk responsibility. Include a brief explanatory note when you send it on.
   - Bin it if it is not important.
   - Never file an item just because you don't know what to do with it.

TOP TIP
The Pareto Principle states that 80% of your performance comes from 20% of your effort. Apply this principle to everything you do and don't spend too much time on any one thing – unless it really warrants it.

Reference

➡ Commonly confused words

➡ Spelling rules

➡ Business thesaurus

Commonly confused words

There are a number of words that can cause confusion in writing. They are words we use regularly. We know what they mean but in the rush and stress of writing at work, we often confuse them. Although these mistakes are common, it will reflect badly on you if you make them. This section will take a look at the most commonly confused words. It will then outline some useful spelling rules. You can also find a useful business thesaurus.

Affect/effect

- Affect is a verb meaning to modify, influence or change
  (e.g. Did the changes affect you?).
- Effect used as a verb means 'to bring about /accomplish'
  (e.g. To effect change is good).
- Effect used as a noun means 'result'
  (e.g. The effect of the meeting was that everyone agreed to work together).

Accept/except

- Accept is a verb meaning 'agree to'
  (e.g. Please accept my apology).
- Except means 'but for'
  (e.g. The office is open everyday except Sunday).

Advice/advise

- Advise is a verb meaning 'inform/counsel'
  (e.g. I advise you to say nothing).
- Advice is a noun meaning 'opinion/judgement'
  (e.g. Take my advice. Do not touch the product).

Alter/altar

- Alter is a verb meaning 'change/modify'
  (e.g. We have to alter the schedule).
- Altar is a raised structure on which to offer sacrifice
  (e.g. He approached the altar).

Allusion/illusion

- Allusion means 'casual reference'
  (e.g. She made an allusion to the remarks made by the boss).
- Illusion means 'deception'
  (e.g. Be under no illusion, the plan will go ahead).

Because/since/due to

- Because implies reason
  (e.g. They spoke to the boss because they were bullied).
- Since implies time
  (e.g. The work plan had been in place since Friday).
- Due to implies cause
  (e.g. Due to the air strike, they could not work).

Between/among

- Between is used when two things or people are involved
  (e.g. They shared the work between the two of them).
- Among is used when three or more are concerned
  (e.g. They shared the sweets among the staff).

Compare with/compare to

- 'Compare with' is used to point out differences between two or more items of reasonable comparison
  (e.g. Compare product X with Product Y).
- 'Compare to' is used to point out or imply resemblances between two or more items not thought of as comparable
  (e.g. 'Shall I compare thee to a summer's morn').

Discreet/discrete

- Discreet means 'on the quiet'.
- Discrete means separate.

E.g./i.e.

- e.g. means for example (from the Latin *exempli gratia*).
- i.e. means that is (from the Latin *id est*), and precedes a redefinition.

Etc.

- Means 'and so forth/and the rest'.
- Etc. should never be used at the end of a list introduced by e.g.

Fewer/smaller/less

- Fewer is for numbers (items that can be counted individually)
  (e.g. There were fewer members present today).
- Smaller is for size
  (e.g. The shoes are smaller).
- Less is for quantities, amounts (volume), or things that differ in degree
  (e.g. They got less orders in May).

Imply/infer

- Imply means to suggest
  (e.g. What are you implying by your remark?).
- Infer means to draw a conclusion
  (e.g. Can I infer from what you say that Mary won't be in?).

Its/it's

- Its denotes possession
  (e.g. The dog wagged its tail).
- It's is the contraction for 'it is'
  (e.g. It's sunny).

Lose/loose

- Lose is when you don't win
  (e.g. They never lose a bid).
- Loose is an adjective meaning untied
  (Be careful; your shoelace is loose).

Stationery/stationary

- Stationery means paper etc.
  (e.g. The stationery cupboard is down the corridor).
- Stationary means not moving
  (e.g. The car was stationary at the time of the crash).

Their/there

- Their means 'belonging to them'
  (e.g. Their work is in project management).
- There means 'that place'
  (e.g. He went there for some fun).

Too/two/to

- Too means 'also' or more than enough, e.g. 'too long'
  (e.g. The team went too; The office is too hot).
- Two is a number
  (e.g. Two hands).
- To denotes direction
  (e.g. We went to the meeting).

Quiet/quite

- Quiet means 'without noise'
  (e.g. The office is quiet).
- Quite means completely, entirely, absolutely
  (e.g. I haven't quite finished).

Spelling rules

Plurals

- Most words are made plural by adding s (e.g. meeting – meetings).
- Words ending in s, ss, ch, sh, x and es form their plural by adding *es* to the end of the word (e.g. bias – bias*es*, fax – fax*es*, watch – watch*es*, boss – boss*es*).
- Words ending in an 'o' preceded by a vowel end their plural in s (e.g. video – videos).
- Words ending in an 'o' preceded by a consonant end their plural in *es* (e.g. potato – potato*es*).
- Words ending in 'y' preceded by a vowel end their plural in s (e.g. holiday – holidays).
- Words ending in 'y' preceded by a consonant end their plural by changing the 'y' to 'i' and adding *es* (e.g. secretary – secretari*es*).
- Some words do not change in the plural (e.g. salmon – salmon).
- Some words have only a plural form (e.g. scissors).

Doubling rule

- One-syllable words with one short vowel and ending in one consonant (e.g. fit), double the final consonant before adding the endings *ing, er* and *ed* (e.g. fit*ting*, fit*ter*, fit*ted*).

Change 'y' to 'i'

- Change the final 'y' to 'i' whenever adding suffixes, unless the suffix begins with 'i' or 'y', or the final 'y' of the baseword has a vowel in front of it (e.g. rely – relied, reliable but relying, play – playing – played – player).

Drop silent 'e'

- Usually drop final silent 'e' on words when adding a suffix beginning with a vowel (e.g. hate – hated, late – later, fame – famous).
- Some words drop the silent 'e' when adding a consonant suffix (e.g. true – truly, due – duly, nine – ninth, argue – argument, whole – wholly, awe – awful).

Spelling 'k'

- Usually spelled 'c' before a, o, u and consonants (e.g. cap, cod, cuff, clap).
- Usually spelled 'k' before i, and e (e.g. kit, keep).
- At the end of a one-syllable word, after one short vowel, 'k' is spelled 'ck' (e.g. clock); after two vowels or a consonant, 'k' is usually spelled 'k' (e.g. look, beak, bank, bark, walk).

'ie' or 'ei'

- Keep the rule in mind: 'i comes before e except after c' (e.g. interview, convenient, friendly but perceived, receive).

Business thesaurus

Adjust

Amend
Calibrate
Fine-tune
Hone
Level
Limit
Mitigate
Modify
Refine
Refocus
Revamp
Scale
Stabilize
Steady
Tune

Assess

Analyze
Ascertain
Audit
Authenticate
Clarify
Compare
Compute
Consider
Contrast
Delve into
Discuss
Evaluate
Examine
Explore
Focus
Hypothesize
Interpret
Investigate
Juxtapose
Model
Qualify
Reconsider
Review
Screen
Scrutinize

Separate
Study
Target
Test
Translate
Weigh

Assign

Appoint
Authorize
Call (to action)
Delegate
Elect
Empower
Enable
Hire
Instruct
Task

Big Change

Change
Convert
Exchange
Migrate
Overhaul
Reengineer
Replace
Shape
Shift
Start over
Substitute
Transform
Transition
Turn

Communicate

Announce
Articulate
Broadcast
Comment
Convey

Convince
Describe
Disclose
Discuss
Engage
Highlight
Inform
Listen
Make aware
Mandate
Negotiate
Notify
Persuade
Position
Present
Publicize
Reinforce
Respond
Share
State
Target
Tell

Compete/Offensive

Attack
Beat
Challenge
Compete
Derail
Dominate
Follow
Lead
Leap-frog
Out-compete
Out-manoeuvre
Out-perform
Overcome
Pre-empt
Prevail
Seize
Surpass
Surprise
Thwart

Transcend
Win
Steer
Supervise

Compete/Defensive

Block
Counter
Defend
Equal
Guard
Hamper
Impede
Meet
Obstruct
Preserve
Protect
Safeguard
Shield
Reduce
Pre-empt
Withstand

Decide

Accept
Advocate
Agree
Approve
Choose
Conclude
Contract
Elect
Endorse
Finalize
Formalize
Formulate
Judge
Prioritize
Recommend
Reject
Sanction
Select

Do

Accomplish
Achieve
Act
Address
Align
Assign
Attain
Build
Compete
Conduct
Consolidate
Coordinate
Deploy
Divest
Ensure
Establish
Execute
Implement
Install
Invest
Move
Operate
Organize
Perform
Pursue
Succeed

Document

Capture
Catalogue
Chart
Compile
Detail
Diagram
Draft
Draw
Draw up
Edit
Format
List
Outline

Print
Publish
Record
Sketch
Summarize
Transcribe
Write

Down/Less

Attenuate
Condense
Consolidate
Constrict
Curtail
Cut (back)
Decrease
Eliminate
Limit
Lower
Minimize
Narrow
Prune
Reduce
Remove
Restrict
Scale down
Shrink
Tighten
Trim
Weaken

Feedback

Audit
Authenticate
Check
Confirm
Learn
Monitor
Observe
Playback
Poll
Prove
Question

Survey
Track
Validate
Verify
Watch

Find

Ask for
Detect
Explore
Identify
Inquire
Inventory
Investigate
Learn
Locate
Observe
Poll
Prompt for
Pursue
Request
Research
Seek
Surface
Survey
Uncover

Fix

Adjust
Correct
Follow up
Improve
Mitigate
Repair
Replace
Resolve
Restore
Tackle

Get

Achieve
Acquire

Attain
Attract
Award
Compile
Concede
Earn
Establish
Extract
Gain
Gather
Obtain
Procure
Purchase
Receive
Recruit
Retain
Secure
Seize
Take

Give

Advance
Afford
Allocate
Assign
Award
Concede
Contribute
Deliver
Deposit
Devote
Distribute
Exchange
Forward
Furnish
Hand (over)
Introduce
Issue
Mail/Ship/File
Present
Send
Supply
Transfer
Transmit

Help

Aid
Alleviate
Assist
Collaborate
Cooperate
Enable
Facilitate
Make easy
Make possible
Partner
Relieve
Serve
Support
Work with

Incremental Change

Adapt
Adjust
Alter
Amend
Balance
Calibrate
Change
Clarify
Fine-tune
Hone
Improve
Level
Massage
Modify
Perfect
Polish
Refine
Revise
Tune

Involve

Bring
Connect
Embrace
Engage

Include
Incorporate
Join
Liaise
Link
Partner
Team
Tie

Keep Doing

Carry through
Commit
Follow through
Keep (doing)
Keep up
Maintain
Preserve
Proceed
Protect
Pursue
Remain
Retain
See through
Sustain
Uphold

Make

Architect
Assemble
Author
Build
Construct
Craft
Create
Design
Develop
Devise
Draft
Form
Formulate
Generate

Model
Mould
Organize
Originate
Plan
Prepare
Produce
Shape
Structure

Manage

Address
Administer
Balance
Control
Direct
Drive
Focus
Govern
Guide
Inspire
Lead
Organize
Oversee
Persuade
Plan
Position
Preside
Recommend
Regulate
Require
Sponsor

Measure

Budget
Calculate
Estimate
Evaluate
Forecast
Predict
Project

Quantify
Track

Meet

Approach
Conduct
Contact
Coordinate
Encounter
Engage
Hold
Include
Interact
Interview
Orient
Schedule
Work with

Motivate

Call (to action)
Encourage
Entice
Excite
Incentivize
Invigorate
Rouse
Stimulate
Support

Plan

Anticipate
Arrange
Chart
Design
Diagram
Formulate
Lay out
Map
Practise
Prepare
Rehearse
Schedule

Political

Arbitrate
Broker
Compromise
Lobby
Manoeuvre
Moderate
Negotiate
Position
Press
Pressure
Re-position

Recommend

Advise
Advocate
Counsel
Encourage
Propose
Suggest
Urge

Sell

Convince
Market
Offer
Persuade
Promote
Propose
Pull
Push

Show

Demonstrate
Establish
Illustrate
Model
Prove
Tour
Validate
Walk-through

Slow Down

Decelerate
Delay
Extend
Lengthen
Limit
Pace
Scale back
Slow
Slow down

Speed Up

Accelerate
Catalyze
Escalate
Expedite
Fast-forward
Fuel
Hasten
Propel
Speed

Start

Accelerate
Begin
Commence
Enter
Establish
Found
Inaugurate
Initiate
Institute
Jump-start
Launch
Move forward
Open
Prepare
Prompt
Ramp-up
Roll-out
Start
Undertake

Stop

Close
Complete
Discontinue
End
Exit
Halt
Leave
Pause
Postpone
Prevent
Ramp-down
Retire
Stop
Suspend
Terminate
Vacate
Wait

Synthesize

Condense
Connect
Consolidate
Distil
Generalize
Include
Incorporate
Link
Merge
Tie
Unify
Unite
Universalize
Weave

Teach

Coach
Counsel
Educate
Inform
Reinforce

Remind
Train

Think Big

Blue-sky
Brainstorm
Conceptualize
Envision
Free-form
Innovate
Invent
Model
Plan
Reshape
Strategize
Transform
Visualize

Try

Attempt
Endeavour
Experiment
Intend
Pilot
Test
Undertake

Understand

Appreciate
Conclude
Confirm
Deduce
Define
Determine
Discriminate
Find out
Frame
Know
Learn
Refute
See

Up/More

Add
Advance
Augment
Broaden
Elevate
Enrich
Exceed
Expand
Heighten
Improve
Increase
Invigorate
Launch
Lift
Maximize
Propagate
Raise
Reinvigorate
Scale-up
Strengthen
Upgrade

Use

Apply
Bring
Employ
Exploit
Lever
Parlay
Process
Target
Transfer
Utilize

Index

OTHER BOOKS TO MAKE YOU BETTER...
Personal Skills

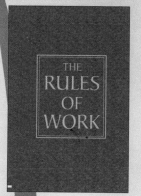

The Rules of Work
A definitive code for personal success
Richard Templar   0 273 66271 6

This is the definitive code for personal success, while remaining a decent person. For the first time, this book reveals the hidden competitive advantage of 10 immutable laws followed by high achievers worldwide. Give yourself the edge at work – learn to play by The Rules.

Get it, and get on.

How to be a Complete and Utter Failure in Life, Work and Everything
39$\frac{1}{2}$ steps to lasting underachievement
Steve McDermott   0 273 66166 3

This is the ultimate "un-improvement" guide, offering 39$\frac{1}{2}$ steps to being a failure using the power of reverse psychology to show you how to be an unqualified success.

How to Manage Your Boss
Developing the perfect working relationship
Ros Jay   0 273 65931 6

Bosses are human – some good, some bad. They have a huge impact on your job satisfaction, your day-to-day happiness, your workload – and yes – your income. If you're lucky they will be understanding, supportive, encouraging and inspiring. Then again they might be lazy, unmotivated, weak, over-emotional, sarcastic, rude, or just downright – well – bossy.

We've all got one. Even the best ones aren't always easy people – and worst case, well, they can make life hell. It's time to learn how to manage them back.

If you wish to find out more about any of these titles visit us at:

www.business-minds.com

Beat Your Goals

the definitive guide to personal success

David Molden & Denise Parker
0 273 65670 8

It's about setting goals that have true meaning and about using all the available resources to become a serial high achiever. It's about removing the hurdles to achieve your aspirations. It's about turning goals into reality!

Coach Yourself

make real change in your life

Anthony M. Grant & Jane Greene
1843 04013 1

Imagine waking up tomorrow morning and your life being exactly how you want it to be. This book will help you help yourself get there. Coaching is a powerful and effective management tool. Imagine the power of knowing how to coach yourself.

Real Coaching and Feedback

how to help people improve their performance

JK Smart
0 273 66328 3

"Reading this book is like somebody switching on the light – suddenly you can see for yourself what you need to do differently. It doesn't tell you what to do, because frankly it's going to be different for everybody and one size doesn't fit all. It triggers the thoughts that let you work it out for yourself. So you create your own solutions, instead of your own problems. And that actually makes you feel good as well as getting the results you want."
– a Real manager

Please visit our website at:

www.business-minds.com